Contents

10	Exclusive Interview with FIFA World Cup™ Legend Pelé
20	Road to Russia
32	The Host Venues
40	FIFA Fan Fest™ – Fun For All Supporters
42	FIFA World Cup™ Words
46	Group A – Russia, Saudi Arabia, Egypt & Uruguay
56	Group B – Portugal, Spain, Morocco & IR Iran
68	Group C – France, Australia, Peru & Denmark
78	Group D – Argentina, Iceland, Croatia & Nigeria
88	The Golden Boot
92	The Host Venues (continued)
96	Group E – Brazil, Switzerland, Costa Rica & Serbia

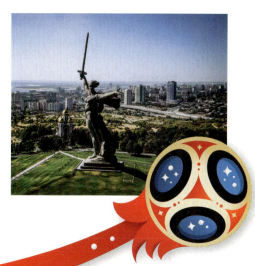

FIFA.com

OFFICIAL 2018 FIFA WORLD CUP™ TOURNAMENT MAGAZINE 3

CONTENTS

106 Group F – Germany, Mexico, Sweden & Korea Republic

118 Group G – Belgium, Panama, Tunisia & England

128 Group H – Poland, Senegal, Colombia & Japan

138 Exclusive Interview with Legend Marcel Desailly

142 The FIFA World Cup™ in Numbers

144 Exclusive Interview with Christian Eriksen

149 A Much-Travelled Trophy

154 88 Years of History

162 The FIFA World Football Museum

168 The Men in the Middle

171 A Marvellous Mascot

172 The Iconic Footballs

175 Test Your Knowledge

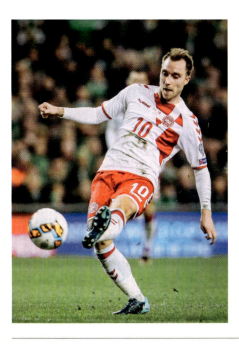

MAGAZINE TEAM

EDITORIAL:
Publication Editor: Roy Gilfoyle
Writers: Chris Brereton, Jon Rayner
Senior Designer: Chris Collins
Designers: Mark Frances, Adam Ward
Special thanks to: Eventica Communications, adidas, the FIFA World Football Museum

TRINITY MIRROR SPORT MEDIA
Managing Director: Steve Hanrahan
Executive Art Editor: Rick Cooke
Executive Editor: Paul Dove
Commercial Director: Will Beedles
Marketing Executive: Claire Brown

PHOTOGRAPHY
Getty Images, PA Images

MANUFACTURED UNDER LICENCE BY:

TRINITY MIRROR SPORT MEDIA

© FIFA, FIFA's Official Licensed Product Logos, and the Emblems, Mascots, Posters and Trophies of the FIFA World Cup™ tournaments are copyrights and/or trademarks of FIFA. All rights reserved.

© Trinity Mirror Sport Media. All rights reserved. No part of this publication may be reproduced without the written permission of the copyright owners. Every effort has been made by the publishers to ensure the accuracy of this publication; the publishers cannot accept responsibility for errors or omissions. Some features in this publication have been written by third-party experts. Any opinions expressed therein are the views of the writers themselves and not necessarily those of FIFA and Trinity Mirror Sport Media.

The publication is produced under a license by FIFA but the content of the publication has not been provided or approved by FIFA. FIFA gives no warranty for the accuracy or completeness of the content or information contained in this publication and disclaims all responsibility and all liability to the fullest extent permissible under applicable law for any expenses, losses, damages and costs which may be incurred by any person in relation to such content or information. Although Trinity Mirror is an appointed licensee by FIFA, the articles contained in this publication are based on Trinity Mirror's independent news gathering and do not necessarily reflect the views of FIFA.

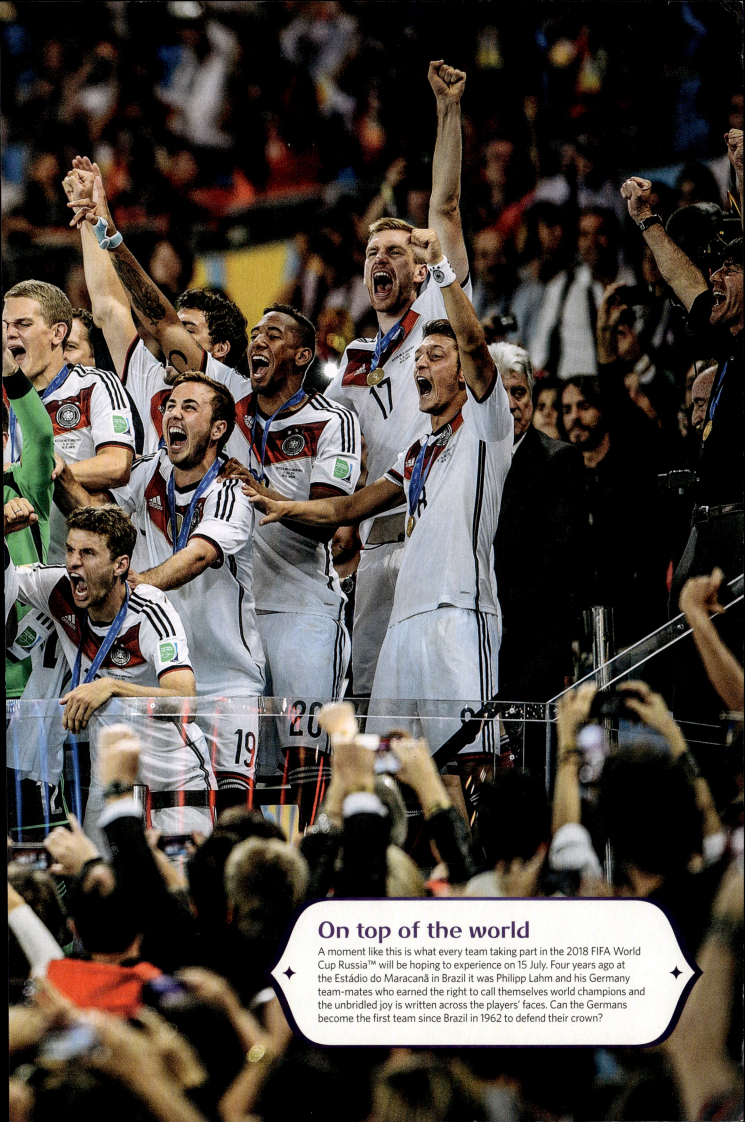

On top of the world

A moment like this is what every team taking part in the 2018 FIFA World Cup Russia™ will be hoping to experience on 15 July. Four years ago at the Estádio do Maracanã in Brazil it was Philipp Lahm and his Germany team-mates who earned the right to call themselves world champions and the unbridled joy is written across the players' faces. Can the Germans become the first team since Brazil in 1962 to defend their crown?

WELCOME

The wait is over, the stage is set

THE WORLD IS WATCHING, EXCITEMENT IS PEAKING. THIRTY-TWO TEAMS ARE PRIMED AND READY TO GO. BRING ON THE 2018 FIFA WORLD CUP RUSSIA™

Very few sporting events across the globe can honestly claim to unite the entire world.

Yet once every four years, a FIFA World Cup™ is held and all eyes fall on the lucky country selected to host the biggest sporting party on Earth.

This year, Russia will host the tournament and three million spectators, sitting in 12 wonderful stadiums for 64 fixtures, will be truly captivated by the football on display.

A further three BILLION people will also watch as the world takes a deep breath, switches on the TV and cheers on its heroes.

The 2018 FIFA World Cup is so full of intriguing storylines and tales of hope that it is difficult to know where to look first.

Can Germany defend their FIFA World Cup crown after their brilliant victory four years ago?

Can England end their 52-year long wait to win their second FIFA World Cup?

Will Cristiano Ronaldo and Lionel Messi continue to shine?

Can Costa Rica again surprise and please the world with a wonderful FIFA World Cup? And will Panama play more of the entertaining football that secured their first-ever FIFA World Cup qualification?

All those questions will be answered in due course in Russia, and the stadiums, the FIFA Fan Fest™ events and the host cities will be overflowing with people enjoying a carnival of sport, friendship and international pride.

The brilliance of the FIFA World Cup will not stop when the final whistle blows on the tournament on 15 July either.

In fact, if anything, the legacy left by the 2018 FIFA World Cup will be just as important as the football itself. A huge upsurge in football coaches and football facilities will mean that this wonderful sport – truly, the world's sport – will become available to millions more children across Russia, thus ensuring that the 2018 FIFA World Cup has a healthy and happy legacy.

The 2018 FIFA World Cup is upon us. Sit back and enjoy a tournament that will capture the world's heart and imagination in equal measure.

THE TRIPLE CHAMPION

ULTIMATE FOOTBALL LEGEND PELÉ TELLS CHRIS BRERETON ABOUT HIS HAT-TRICK OF FIFA WORLD CUP™ WINS – AND PINPOINTS THE THREE PLAYERS TO WATCH IN 2018

He is the first name on everybody's lips and the first name on everybody's list.

Football is renowned for provoking and creating fierce debate, and no other sport can match its capacity for discussion and arguments about who is the strongest, the fastest, the most ruthless, the most passionate.

Yet one man manages to unite the whole world, and silence all arguments, when the question is asked about who is the greatest footballer ever to lace up a pair of boots and walk onto a pitch at a FIFA World Cup™.

That person, that legend, is Edson Arantes do Nascimento.

That person, that legend, is Pelé.

The 77-year-old's FIFA World Cup history is the benchmark for glory and longevity, and his name has become synonymous with success, footballing excellence and a sheer love for the sport that has given him so much.

Pelé first played in, and won, a FIFA World Cup in 1958 when he exploded onto the world stage with a series of performances that were so technically excellent and so visually beautiful that they have resonated down the six decades since.

Until 1958, Brazil had been close to FIFA World Cup glory but not close enough. They lost the deciding match to Uruguay on home soil in 1950, they had come third in 1938, and they were by no means favourites in Sweden 60 years ago. A disappointing quarter-final loss to Hungary in 1954 did little to boost Brazil's confidence either.

Yet Pelé, alongside fellow genius Garrincha, changed Brazil's FIFA World Cup story and set him on the road to greatness.

Pelé shows the Jules Rimet Cup™ to the people of Paris

"For me, everything was new," Pelé said, when looking back at that first FIFA World Cup win.

"It was like a dream. At that World Cup I was just 17, I had never travelled by plane before and when we arrived in Sweden, nobody knew anything about us, nobody felt we would become world champions. But Brazil became known worldwide."

They certainly did. At the time, Pelé was the youngest player ever to feature in a FIFA World Cup and his six goals put him on the path to tournament immortality. A hat-trick against France in the semi-final helped Brazil into a showdown against host nation Sweden. Pelé scored two goals in a 5-2 victory, with one goal in particular being a moment of beauty as he flicked the ball over a defender inside the area before volleying past Swedish goalkeeper Karl Svensson, a goal Pelé himself claims as one of his best FIFA World Cup goals ever.

"I can still see the King of Sweden coming onto the field at the end to greet us after we had won," he recalls, before modestly sharing the praise among his fellow Brazilian players.

"For me, Garrincha was the best but Zito and Didi were also very important to us.

"All the way through my career, I had players whom I admired. It is very difficult to name one. With me there was Zito and Garrincha but there were also great players like Franz Beckenbauer

> "All the way through my career, I had players that I admired. It is very difficult to name one. With me there was Zito and Garrincha but there were also great players like Franz Beckenbauer."

Garrincha

Brazil's 1970 FIFA World Cup heroes

Pelé and Gerson share a moment of joy after success in the 1970 FIFA World Cup

EXCLUSIVE INTERVIEW

and many others. Our manager, Mario Zagallo, was also without a doubt the best manager I played for."

The aforementioned Garrincha was just as impressive four years after the Sweden tournament when Brazil won their second consecutive FIFA World Cup, although Pelé's own joy at winning the event was tempered by an injury that brought his involvement to a premature end.

1966 came and went as Sir Alf Ramsay's 'Wingless Wonders' England team won the tournament on home soil before Pelé truly cemented his reputation in Mexico in 1970 at a FIFA World Cup that seemed especially bright and vivid, and not just because colour television was becoming the norm.

Brazil, led by the strong, quick, powerful man Pelé had become, were simply breathtaking, winning the tournament with a 4-1 victory over Italy in a spectacle that has become the benchmark for exciting and iconic performances.

Yet despite lifting the Official Trophy for the third time in 1970 – the only man in history to have done so – Pelé laughs when he discusses what he remembers most about Mexico.

It is not his four goals in the tournament, or Carlos Alberto's wonderful strike in the final against Italy, nor the gigantic 100,000+ crowds who filled the steaming hot Estadio Azteca

stadium in Mexico City. No, if anything, it's Pelé's 'failings' that he looks back on with a wry smile.

"There are two moments that are commented on more than us winning in 1970," he said.

"Gordon Banks' wonderful save from my header in our group match and when I tried to lob Czechoslovakia goalkeeper Ivo Viktor from inside my own half. Both efforts missed but I get asked about them more than anything else!"

Pelé retired from Brazil duty the year after the 1970 FIFA World Cup success and his time since has seen him pour his efforts and attention into all manner of charitable causes, including being appointed a UNESCO Goodwill Ambassador, and he has also been instrumental in trying to reduce world poverty and hunger.

Yet, without a doubt, football and the FIFA World Cup are what excite him the most. He cannot wait for the tournament to begin and he believes the host nation stands a fantastic chance of going all the way.

"In Russia, Russia itself will benefit because they will be playing at home. They are a very disciplined team and I think they can be champions," he said. "I also think Germany will be strong and from the Americas, Argentina are a good team – but Brazil will also be among the favourites.

Brazil and (below left) Germany will be among the favourites

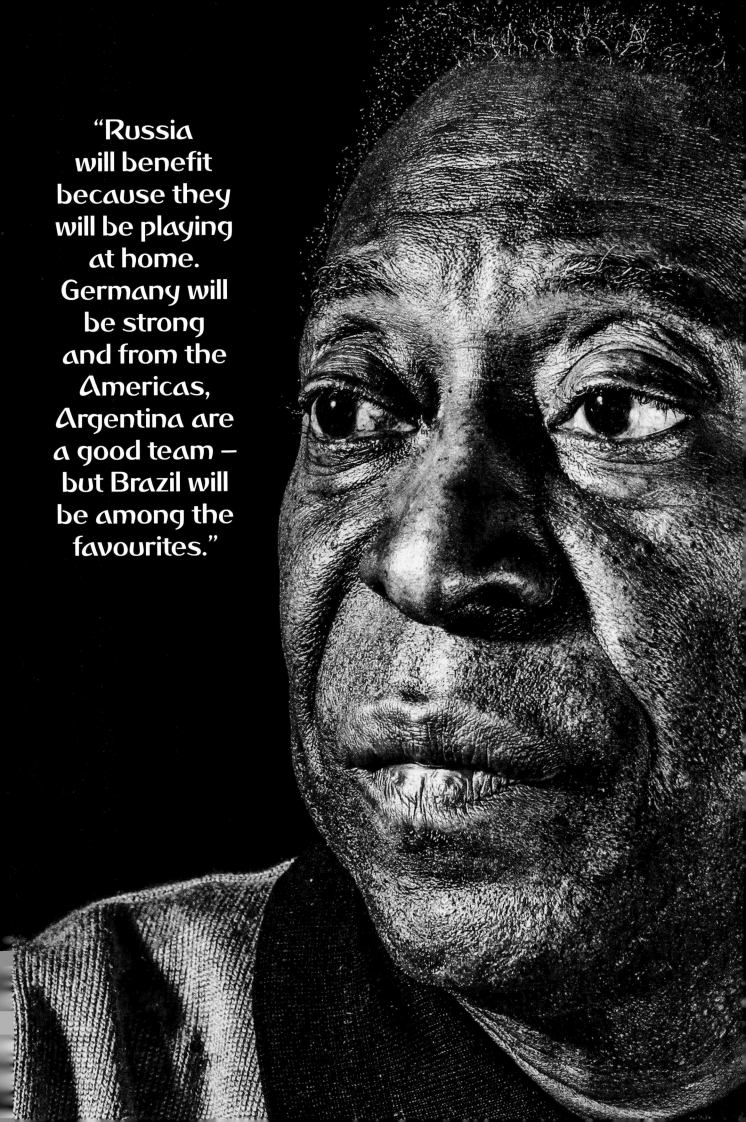

"Russia will benefit because they will be playing at home. Germany will be strong and from the Americas, Argentina are a good team – but Brazil will be among the favourites."

Messi, Ronaldo and Neymar (below) are the best in the world at the moment, according to Pelé

EXCLUSIVE INTERVIEW

> "When it comes to players, I think at the moment the best three are Lionel Messi, Cristiano Ronaldo and Neymar but they cannot really be compared. They cannot compare because they all perform different functions with different characteristics."

"In the last World Cup we had the best players in the world but the team was disorganised. It seems that now we'll have a team and a Seleção that gives us confidence."

Pelé is interested in far more, though, than simply hoping Brazil can lift the Official Trophy for the sixth time, and the entire event is also exciting the man known simply by his nickname.

In particular, he cannot wait to see Russia come together as one to provide superb footballing memories across the 12 stadiums.

He is also eager to witness the plethora of wonderful football talent on display and he has his own thoughts on who will light up the 2018 FIFA World Cup.

"The Russians love football, just as the Brazilians do, and they deserve this World Cup," Pelé said. "When it comes to players, I think at the moment the best three are Lionel Messi, Cristiano Ronaldo and Neymar but they cannot really be compared. They are different because Cristiano is a finisher, a striker, and Messi is more of a playmaker. They cannot compare because they all perform different functions with different characteristics."

With three FIFA World Cup victories under his belt and a reputation that could not get any higher among football fans across the globe, Pelé is clear about how much joy football has brought to his life – none more so than when representing his country at the highest level.

"I never had disappointments," he says. "I was a bit bruised by 1966 but that is it. The most important thing is that I'm able to say I was a world champion three times."

Indeed, that is the most important thing and it proves that no matter how famous, successful or well-known you become, a footballer's first desire is silverware, national acclaim and a place in the history books.

And a whole new generation now has the chance to emulate the greatest of them all and write their own glorious futures in Russia this summer.

PICTURE POWER

Was it or wasn't it?

You can tell by the reaction of the England players that it was! The question, of course, was about whether the ball had crossed the goal line following a shot from Geoff Hurst in extra time of the 1966 FIFA World Cup™ final between England and West Germany at Wembley. The Russian linesman adjudged the ball had crossed the line, England went 3-2 up, and went on to win 4-2 with Hurst completing the only ever FIFA World Cup™ final hat-trick.

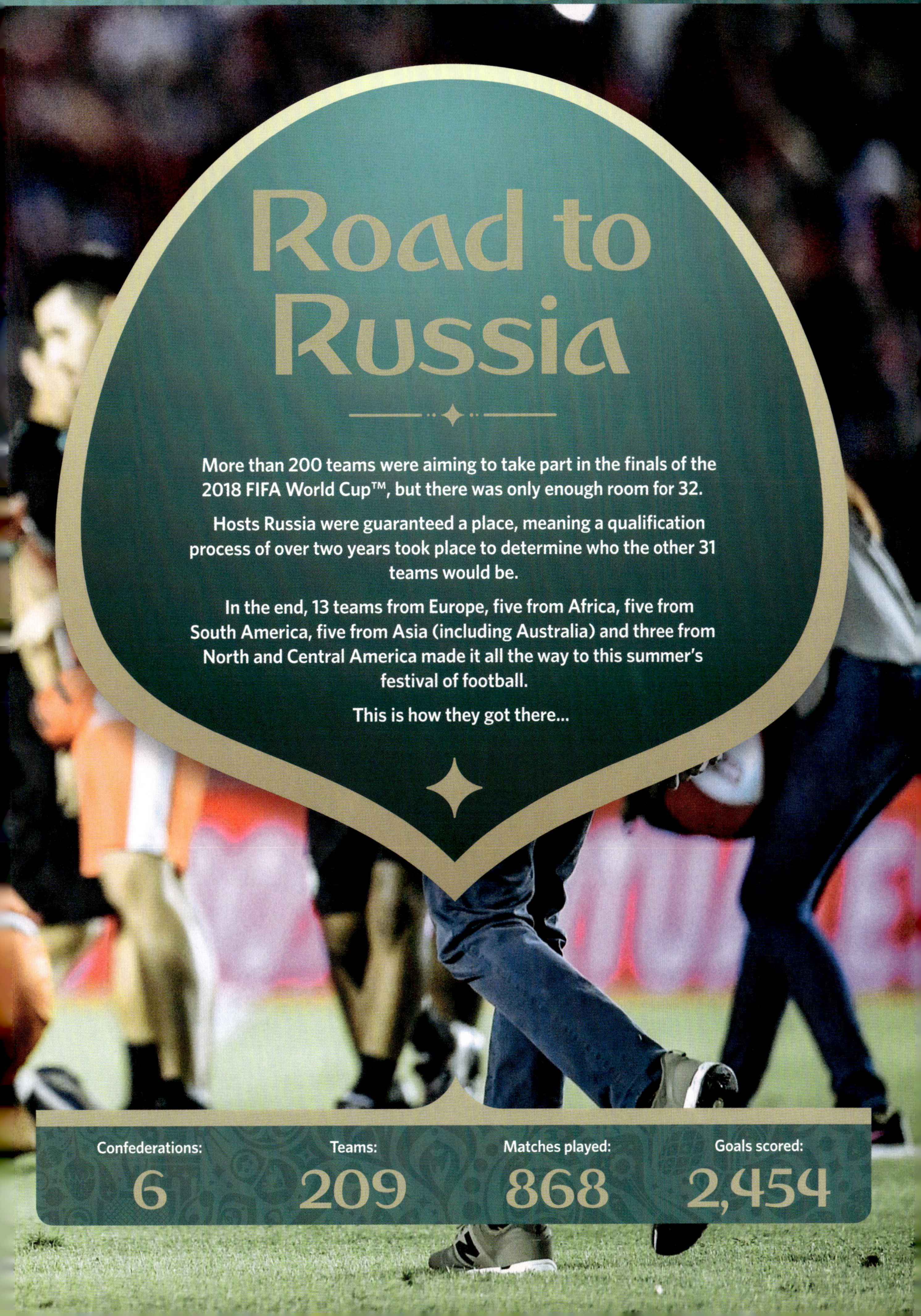

Road to Russia

More than 200 teams were aiming to take part in the finals of the 2018 FIFA World Cup™, but there was only enough room for 32.

Hosts Russia were guaranteed a place, meaning a qualification process of over two years took place to determine who the other 31 teams would be.

In the end, 13 teams from Europe, five from Africa, five from South America, five from Asia (including Australia) and three from North and Central America made it all the way to this summer's festival of football.

This is how they got there...

Confederations: **6**

Teams: **209**

Matches played: **868**

Goals scored: **2,454**

Road to Russia

Europe

There were 13 qualification places up for grabs when competition began in Europe in September 2016.

Nine group winners would book their places at the 2018 FIFA World Cup™ in Russia, with the eight best runners-up taking part in four play-off matches to decide the other four qualifiers.

World champions Germany led the way in the group phase, winning all ten of their matches, while the tightest group saw both Portugal and Switzerland win nine out of ten games to finish on 27 points each, with the Portuguese edging through.

France, Serbia, Poland, England, Spain, Belgium and Iceland also topped their groups, the latter becoming the smallest nation, in terms of population, to ever reach the World Cup finals.

The play-offs saw dramatic qualification routes for Switzerland, Croatia, Sweden and Denmark.

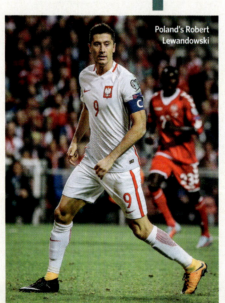

Poland's Robert Lewandowski

TEAMS QUALIFIED:

- Belgium
- Croatia
- Denmark
- England
- France
- Germany
- Iceland
- Poland
- Portugal
- Serbia
- Spain
- Sweden
- Switzerland

Iceland celebrate

QUALIFYING STATS

Matches played:	Goals scored:	Most goals – team:	Most goals – player:
278	807	43 Germany & Belgium	16 Robert Lewandowski - Poland

Road to Russia

South America

Probably the most straightforward of the FIFA World Cup™ qualification routes takes place in South America.

Ten teams played each other twice over a two-year period up to October 2017, with the top four teams qualifying for the finals in Russia.

The team that finished fifth – on this occasion, Peru – went into a play-off round with Oceania qualifiers New Zealand, with the Peruvians coming through.

Despite an early scare, five-time winners Brazil cruised through qualifying, topping the group by ten points. Chile beat the Brazilians in their first qualifying match but the *Copa América* champions ultimately finished sixth and were eliminated.

The same fate almost befell two-time winners Argentina, who came into the final group match in sixth place after a stuttering campaign. A 3-1 win in Ecuador, however, saw them leap up to third just behind fellow qualifiers Uruguay, and one ahead of Colombia.

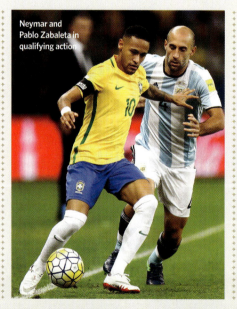

Neymar and Pablo Zabaleta in qualifying action

TEAMS QUALIFIED:

Argentina
Brazil
Colombia

Peru
Uruguay

Uruguay's Edinson Cavani after scoring against Brazil

QUALIFYING STATS

Matches played: **90**

Goals scored: **242**

Most goals – team: **41** Brazil

Most goals – player: **10** Edinson Cavani - Uruguay

"We'll be in good shape when we get to Russia because we're still growing. The team is going to get rid of all the tension and fear it felt in qualifying."
— Lionel Messi (Argentina)

Road to Russia

Africa

After 127 matches stretching back to October 2015, 53 teams were whittled down to five triumphant African nations.

Round one of qualifying saw the lowest-ranked African nations battle it out for a second knockout phase against the higher-ranked countries. Forty teams were then reduced to 20, all of which were placed in five groups of four.

The winners of the groups qualified for the 2018 FIFA World Cup Russia™.

Group A was won by Tunisia, who edged out Congo DR, with Nigeria finishing five points clear at the top of Group B.

Morocco finished above Côte d'Ivoire in Group C despite three 0-0 draws in their six group matches, while Senegal clinched their spot in Russia by winning their penultimate game, against South Africa, to top Group D.

Egypt complete Africa's fab five. Despite being the only table-topping side to lose a group match, they finished four points ahead of Uganda in Group E.

Sadio Mané in action for Senegal

TEAMS QUALIFIED:

- Egypt
- Morocco
- Nigeria
- Senegal
- Tunisia

Nigeria's players celebrate

QUALIFYING STATS

Matches played:	Goals scored:	Most goals – team:	Most goals – player:
127	315	19 Congo DR	5 Mohamed Salah - *Egypt* Préjuce Nakoulma - *Burkina Faso*

26 OFFICIAL 2018 FIFA WORLD CUP™ TOURNAMENT MAGAZINE

"I have the honour to play for the Egyptian national team. The flag of my country will always have a special place in my heart."

— Mohamed Salah
(Egypt)

Road to Russia

Asia

The teams that qualified for the 2018 FIFA World Cup™ had to go through up to five qualifying rounds to make it to Russia.

Round one saw the lowest-ranked teams from the continent battle it out to join the remaining 34 teams in round two, where they were split into eight groups.

The eight group winners and four best-placed runners-up moved through to another group stage in round three, where there were two groups of six.

The teams that finished first and second in both groups – IR Iran, Korea Republic, Japan and Saudi Arabia – qualified for the 2018 FIFA World Cup™ while the two third-place teams went into round four, which was a play-off between Syria and Australia.

Australia needed a second-leg extra-time goal to win, which put them into a CONCACAF-AFC play-off with Honduras. The Socceroos won 3-1 on aggregate to become the 31st team to book their place at this summer's finals.

Australia won a play-off against Honduras

TEAMS QUALIFIED:

- Australia
- IR Iran
- Japan

- Saudi Arabia
- Korea Republic

IR Iran and Korea Republic both qualified from their group

QUALIFYING STATS

Matches played: 226

Goals scored: 665

Most goals – team: 48 *Australia*

Most goals – player: 16
Mohammad Al-Sahlawi - *Saudi Arabia*
Ahmed Khalil - *United Arab Emirates*

"If we want to get to the second round, we need to be fitter and better prepared than the other teams. It's important to finish the season well and be high on confidence."

— Son Heung-Min (Korea Republic)

Road to Russia

North & Central America and the Caribbean

A long campaign saw the region's lowest-ranked teams go through three qualifying rounds, after which six teams emerged to take on the six highest-ranked countries.

Twelve teams were divided into three groups, which produced three winners and three runners-up to go into one final group.

The top three teams from that group – Mexico, Costa Rica and Panama – advanced to the 2018 FIFA World Cup™, with the team in fourth going into an intercontinental play-off. That team was Honduras, but they lost out to Australia.

TEAMS QUALIFIED:

- Costa Rica
- Mexico
- Panama

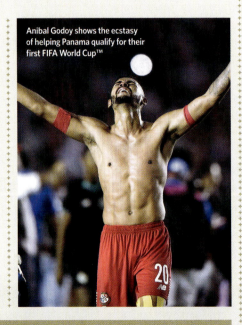

Anibal Godoy shows the ecstasy of helping Panama qualify for their first FIFA World Cup™

QUALIFYING STATS

Matches played:	Goals scored:	Most goals – team:	Most goals – player:
112	319	37 USA	9 Carlos Ruiz - Guatemala

Oceania

Two qualifying rounds reduced 11 teams to six qualifiers, all of which went into two groups of three.

The teams that topped those groups – New Zealand and the Solomon Islands – then had a play-off to decide which team would represent Oceania in an intercontinental play-off.

New Zealand beat the Solomon Islands but were then overcome by Peru.

New Zealand reached a play-off before losing out to Peru

QUALIFYING STATS

Matches played:	Goals scored:
35	106

Most goals – team:	Most goals – player:
24 New Zealand	8 Chris Wood New Zealand

"I'm proud to have a shot at a fourth World Cup. What's still the same is my hunger, my drive to win both individually and as a team. That's what's kept me at the highest level."

— Andres Guardado (Mexico)

Welcome to Russia

Russia simply cannot wait for the 2018 FIFA World Cup™ to begin.

While the bidding process and preparations for this event may have lasted just a few years, in reality the Russian people have been desperate to host football's biggest occasion for decades.

Russia actually found out it had won the right to host the 2018 FIFA World Cup™ back in December 2010, and that is when the work really began to create a spectacle that would impress the world. And there is a lot the world will be impressed by.

Watching the tournament on television will give fans a flavour of Russia, but those who visit this enormous country will find a nation rich in history, beauty and ambition.

While all of Russia's host cities are located in the west of the country, its landmass extends across 11 time zones, making it the biggest country on Earth, even if its 140 million population is only the ninth highest in the world.

That population is diverse though, with 140 nationalities speaking over 100 different languages.

The landscape is wonderful and full of variety. From the snow-capped peaks of the Ural and Caucasus mountains, to the Siberian forests and meandering rivers – including Europe's longest, the Volga – as well as the deserts and grasslands of its central steppe, its beauty is simply breathtaking!

Russia has also made an immense contribution to the world's culture, arts and sciences down the years, having produced more than 20 Nobel Prize winners, including 20th century poets Boris Pasternak and Joseph Brodsky, scientist and human rights activist Andrei Sakharov, and the first President of the USSR, Mikhail Gorbachev.

Russia also enjoys a strong tradition in music, literature and arts. The Bolshoi in Moscow and the Mariinsky Theatre in Saint Petersburg are world-renowned opera and ballet brands.

It is a country rich in natural resources and it also has a sporting heritage that makes its people proud and makes them desperate to welcome the world's top players to its doorstep.

They have already opened their doors to the 1980 Summer Olympics and the 2014 Winter Olympics but now they are ready to host the 2018 FIFA World Cup™ in 12 stadiums in 11 host cities that will make football's superstars feel right at home.

Venues

Kaliningrad Stadium, Kaliningrad	Luzhniki Stadium, Moscow
Volgograd Arena, Volgograd	Samara Arena, Samara
Ekaterinburg Arena, Ekaterinburg	Rostov Arena, Rostov-on-Don
Fisht Stadium, Sochi	Spartak Stadium, Moscow
Nizhny Novgorod Stadium, Nizhny Novgorod	Saint Petersburg Stadium, Saint Petersburg
Kazan Arena, Kazan	Mordovia Arena, Saransk

Kaliningrad Stadium

Host City: Kaliningrad
Project: New stadium
Location: Oktyabrsky Island
Home Team: FC Baltika Kaliningrad

DEVELOPMENT
Kaliningrad Stadium has been built for the 2018 FIFA World Cup Russia™ on Oktyabrsky Island, right in the heart of Kaliningrad. The selection of Kaliningrad as a host city prompted the local authorities to develop the island, which for many centuries had been a wilderness, left largely untouched. FC Baltika Kaliningrad will play their home games here after the tournament.

DESIGN
Kaliningrad Stadium is a multi-purpose arena. As well as football matches, it hosts other sporting events and concerts. After the 2018 FIFA World Cup™, a new residential development will be built around the stadium, with parks, quays and embankments alongside the Pregola River.

CITY
Founded in the 13th century by knights of the Teutonic Order and formerly known as Königsberg, the capital of East Prussia, Kaliningrad is home to over 450,000 people and an important Russian Baltic seaport and gateway to Europe. The region has been known from classical antiquity as a main source of amber in Europe. Around 90 per cent of the world's amber deposits are located here.

Volgograd Arena

Host City: Volgograd
Project: New stadium
Location: Central Park
Home Team: FC Rotor

DEVELOPMENT
Volgograd Arena has been built on the site of the old Central Stadium, at the foot of the Mamayev Kurgan war memorial. The location of the previous stadium is a Mecca for local football supporters, with the more seasoned among them able to remember European victory over Manchester United and domestic battles with Spartak Moscow.

DESIGN
The stadium's façade takes the form of an inverted, truncated cone with an open lattice structure. The stadium's roof has been constructed in a special way with cables reminiscent of the spokes of the wheel on a bicycle.

CITY
Formerly known as Stalingrad, Volgograd extends alongside the Volga River and has one million residents. Volgograd and the surrounding area saw some of the heaviest battles during World War II. Volgograd is now a centre for ecotourism in Russia.

Ekaterinburg Arena

DEVELOPMENT
Home to one of the country's oldest football clubs, FC Ural, this stadium was built in 1953. Since then, it has been refurbished on a number of occasions. The last of these refits was completed in 2011. On each occasion, however, the stadium's historical façade remained untouched as an architectural legacy.

DESIGN
The stadium has retained its recognisable look although a roof and temporary stands have been installed for Russia 2018. FC Ural will benefit from all of these improvements as they will continue to play their home games here after the tournament.

CITY
Located on the geographical border of Europe and Asia, and at the foot of the Ural Mountains, Ekaterinburg has a population of 1.4 million. The city was founded by a decree of Peter the Great in 1723. Ekaterinburg is the fourth largest city in Russia. During the 18th century, the city became known as Russia's iron-making centre, and it is now a modern city with world-class infrastructure.

Host City: Ekaterinburg
Project: Stadium reconstruction
Location: Repin Street
Home team: FC Ural

Fisht Stadium

DEVELOPMENT
Located in the Olympic Park in Imeretin Valley in Sochi, Fisht Stadium was built for the Winter Olympics in 2014. For the FIFA World Cup™, there are temporary stands behind each goal. In future, the national team will hold training camps here and play matches at the stadium.

DESIGN
Fisht Stadium was originally named after Mount Fisht, a peak in the Caucasus range of mountains. In the local language, Adygeyan, "fisht" means "white head". The silhouette of the arena, which was designed by British architects, resembles a snow-capped mountain peak.

CITY
The Black Sea resort of Sochi rose to global prominence after being awarded the 2014 Olympic Winter Games. Situated along 140km of the coast (the longest city in Europe), this resort is one of Russia's most popular tourist destinations and a truly great sports city.

Host City: Sochi
Project: Stadium reconstruction
Location: Olympic Park, Adler district
Home team: Russia

Kazan Arena

Host City:
Kazan

Project:
New stadium

Location:
Chistopolskaya Street, Novo-Savinovsky district

Home team:
FC Rubin Kazan

DEVELOPMENT
Kazan Arena was built for the Summer World University Games in 2013, when it hosted the opening and closing ceremonies. A football pitch was installed once the games were over. The stadium hosted its first match in August 2013, between Rubin Kazan and Lokomotiv Moscow. The stadium has also hosted the World Aquatics Championships, plus concerts and cultural events.

DESIGN
Kazan Arena was designed by the firm of architects behind Wembley Stadium and Emirates Stadium in London. It has a unique design, which blends into Kazan's urban landscape. Viewed from above, the arena, which stands on the banks of the Kazanka River, resembles a water lily.

CITY
Kazan is one of the oldest Russian cities and celebrated its millennium in 2005. Modern Kazan is the capital of the Republic of Tatarstan and is home to 1.2 million residents. While history is an important part of its identity, Kazan is also a city of youth, home to 30 of Russia's largest universities and more than 180,000 students. The 16th-century Kazan Kremlin is a UNESCO World Heritage site.

Nizhny Novgorod Stadium

Host City:
Nizhny Novgorod

Project:
New stadium

Location:
confluence of the Oka and Volga rivers

Home team:
Olympiets Nizhny Novgorod

DEVELOPMENT
Nizhny Novgorod Stadium is situated in one of the city's most picturesque locations at the confluence of the Volga and Oka rivers, near the Alexander Nevsky Cathedral from where there is a wonderful view of the Nizhny Novgorod Kremlin on the other side of the Oka. After Russia 2018, the stadium will be home to local club Olympiets Nizhny Novgorod.

DESIGN
Nizhny Novgorod Stadium's design was inspired by aspects of nature in the Volga region – water and wind. At the same time, given its location near the city's most historic districts, the building is understated to blend into its surroundings.

CITY
Due to its advantageous location on the Volga River, Nizhny Novgorod developed into Russia's key commerce centre in the 19th century. It is one of Russia's most traditional and beautiful cities. Nizhny Novgorod is one of a hundred world cities included on the UNESCO World Heritage List.

FAN FEST

The place to be

EXCITEMENT AND FUN GUARANTEED AT THE FIFA FAN FEST™

If you want to celebrate a win with friends, console opposition supporters if they have lost, or if you simply want to experience the international fun and spirit that is always on display at a FIFA World Cup™, then you should definitely head to one place: a FIFA Fan Fest™ venue.

Fans from all over the globe will convene in Russia for the 2018 FIFA World Cup™, with 11 host cities across Russia opening their arms to welcome supporters from all 32 nations taking part.

Fans who head to a FIFA Fan Fest can expect plenty of charm, celebrations, cheering and excitement, and apart from being in a stadium itself, a FIFA Fan Fest will provide the best spectator interaction and excitement a football fan can get.

The FIFA Fan Fest first saw the light of day at the 2006 FIFA World Cup™ in Germany and since then, over 30 million people have attended an event. Those making their way to a Fan Fest in Russia will have 11 unique locations in which they can come together to admire both the football and their surroundings.

Spots like Sparrow Hills on the right bank of the Moskva River in Moscow, Konyyshennaya Square in Saint Petersburg and the Armi Embankment in Volgograd have all been chosen to take the fans' breath away and provide a great day's entertainment.

All Fan Fest areas will be free to enter and will host musicians from across the planet as well as interactive games for children and the best screens to catch all the on-pitch action.

"The FIFA Fan Fest will be the perfect opportunity for each of our host cities to show the world their unique culture and friendly hospitality. These venues will serve as informal and joyful meeting points, from where I am sure fans will take some of their best memories from the amazing event," said 2018 FIFA World Cup Local Organising Committee CEO, Alexey Sorokin.

The enjoyment shown by fans from across the globe at the 2014 FIFA World Cup in Brazil was one of the highlights of the entire tournament – and now it is Russia's turn to show supporters that the FIFA Fan Fest is the place to be.

FIFA WORLD CUP™ WORDS

What players and coaches from around the world have been saying...

"It is the first time I have qualified for a World Cup and I am so, so happy."

Victor Lindelöf
(Sweden)

"We are not going to Russia just to be competitive. I want to win our matches."

Bert van Marwijk
(Australia coach)

"We have a physical presence up front but we also have players with good technical ability. The extraordinary skills of Christian Eriksen give us something extra in that respect."

Åge Hareide
(Denmark coach)

"I'm thrilled about the World Cup because I'd already missed out on one due to injury, but a lot of work still needs to be done. It's special because of the work carried out by this national team for the past year and a half, and through sacrifice and hard work, we qualified earlier than planned."

Thiago Alcantara
(Spain)

"Germany, Spain, Brazil, France and Argentina are going to be the favourites. Despite the fact that Portugal won't be included among the favourites, we always compete and will do so again."

Cristiano Ronaldo
(Portugal)

"We're quite a young team. We don't have huge experience of tournament football, but as a team we have a lot of potential and a team that we think will improve in the next few years."

— Gareth Southgate (England Coach)

"I am extremely delighted to qualify for the World Cup, which we hope will be Nigeria's best in terms of record and performance."

— Ogenyi Onazi (Nigeria)

"I told the group 'Messi did not owe the World Cup to Argentina, but football owed the World Cup to Messi. We should help him be there.'"

— Jorge Sampaoli (Argentina coach)

"It is always a challenge for us to play against the world's best teams and we must give our all if we are to reach the second stage. But we should set new goals to achieve better results than before. For me, I should do my best to make it into our World Cup team."

— Takuma Asano (Japan)

"I want us to boss matches, whoever and wherever we're playing. And we intend to give our all to bring our fans joy, because they deserve it."

— Ricardo Gareca (Peru coach)

"We have a great generation of players. Everyone plays for the team and it's more than just the 11 players on the pitch. We've got 23 or 24 players ready to go out there and give their all. The coach believes in us, which gives us the energy we need to succeed at the World Cup."

— Wahbi Khazri (Tunisia)

"We're a strong unit, and not just on the pitch: we're one family with one objective, which is to raise the profile of Egypt and Egyptian football. We want to do it and put a smile on the faces of tens of millions of people."

— Essam El Hadary (Egypt)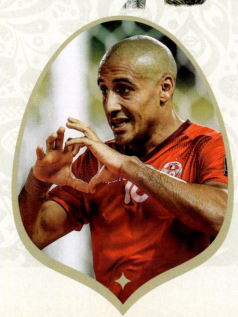

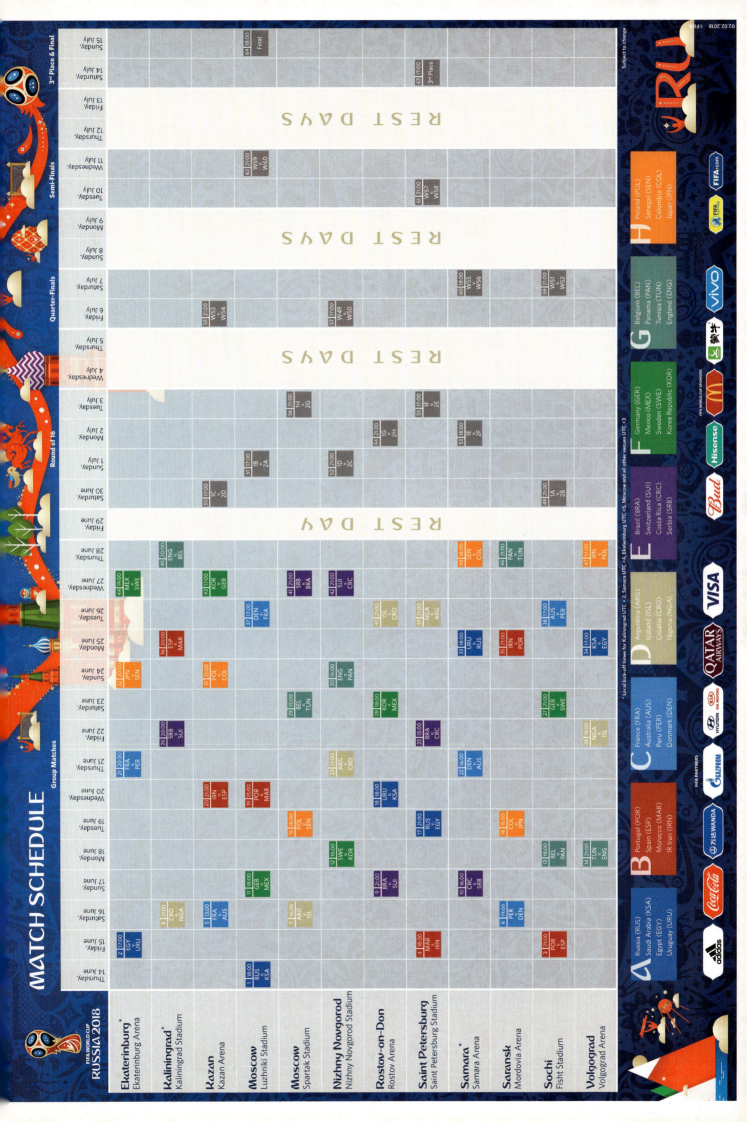

RUSSIA

SAUDI ARABIA

EGYPT

URUGUAY

FIFA WORLD CUP RUSSIA 2018

Group A Fixtures

14 JUNE
Russia v. Saudi Arabia
16:00
Luzhniki Stadium, Moscow

15 JUNE
Egypt v. Uruguay
13:00
Ekaterinburg Arena, Ekaterinburg

19 JUNE
Russia v. Egypt
19:00
Saint Petersburg Stadium, Saint Petersburg

20 JUNE
Uruguay v. Saudi Arabia
16:00
Rostov Arena, Rostov-on-Don

25 JUNE
Saudi Arabia v. Egypt
15:00
Volgograd Arena, Volgograd

25 JUNE
Uruguay v. Russia
15:00
Samara Arena, Samara

Kick-offs are UK time (UTC/GMT)

OFFICIAL 2018 FIFA WORLD CUP™ TOURNAMENT MAGAZINE 47

GROUP A
Russia
Saudi Arabia
Egypt
Uruguay

RUSSIA

The pressure is on Russia as they host the 2018 FIFA World Cup™ with the aim of ensuring that they give the home fans plenty to get excited about.

Russia's history in the FIFA World Cup™ is chequered but there are plenty of highlights in their major tournament history to give hope that they can live with the best teams on the planet.

Back when they were part of the USSR, their first attempt at winning the FIFA World Cup came in 1958 when they reached the quarter-finals and those early days were quite consistent, as they reached the same stage in two of the next three tournaments.

In the middle of those quarter-final finishes came their best ever FIFA World Cup performance in 1966. In that tournament they topped a group containing Italy, Chile and North Korea and beat Hungary in the quarter-finals before being edged out by West Germany in the semis as they finished fourth.

Since then, they have been regular qualifiers for FIFA World Cup finals tournaments without making a major impact, especially since the break-up of the Soviet Union in 1991.

The European Championships have been a more productive competition over the years.

The Soviet Union won the first competition, back in 1960, beating Yugoslavia in the final.

Since then, they have appeared in three finals, in 1964, 1972 and 1988, only to be beaten on each occasion.

Their best recent performance was in 2008 when they reached the semi-finals before losing out to Spain. This year, with the eyes of the world's biggest nation on them, Russia will be desperate to deliver.

> "In my opinion, Uruguay is the favourite in our group. There are no simple rivals at the World Cup."
> — Fyodor Smolov

HOW THEY QUALIFIED

Put simply, as hosts they didn't need to qualify!

Given they were already guaranteed a place in their home FIFA World Cup, Russia have spent the last few years playing friendly matches and building a team capable of taking on the world's best and making their country proud.

Coached by Stanislav Cherchesov, their programme has included matches against teams from several different continents as they bid to experience as many types of opponent as possible.

They also hosted the FIFA Confederations Cup in 2017 in which they beat New Zealand 2-0, but lost to European champions Portugal 1-0 and Mexico 2-1, thus failing to qualify for the semi-finals.

Their other recent matches have included high-profile friendlies with the likes of Korea DPR, Argentina and Spain. The most encouraging of those came when they drew 3-3 with the Spanish, having been 2-0 down.

Russia
Saudi Arabia
Egypt
Uruguay

GROUP **A**

FIFA WORLD CUP RUSSIA 2018

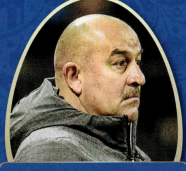

THE COACH

STANISLAV CHERCHESOV

Stanislav Cherchesov was brought in as manager of the Russian national team two years ago with one aim: to help the squad satisfy home expectations at the 2018 FIFA World Cup.

Cherchesov was recruited from Legia Warsaw, having led them to the league and cup double in Poland.

He is a former Russian international goalkeeper, having played 39 times for his country, and had spells with several clubs in Austria, Germany and Russia, including four stints with Spartak Moscow.

His managerial career has taken him to Austria, Russia and Poland and his nation will hope they have a man in charge who can help his players realise their potential.

"We experienced the fans' support at the Confederations Cup and it seems that our bond with them has got even stronger in recent outings. We hope we can win over even more fans in the build-up to the World Cup."

ALL-TIME TOP GOALSCORER
OLEG BLOKHIN
42

ALL-TIME MOST CAPS
SERGEI IGNASHEVICH
120

HAT-TRICK OF HEROES

IGOR AKINFEEV

Russia's goalkeeper and captain is the ultimate one-club man.

Having spent his youth career with CSKA Moscow, he went on to make his debut for the first team at the age of 16 and, befitting his career, he kept a clean sheet and saved a penalty in a 2-0 win.

Since then his career has been a tale of consistency and achievement as he has gone on to claim six Russian league titles, six Russian Cups and one UEFA Cup.

His international recognition began when he was only 18 in 2004 and he now has over 100 caps, having won the Lev Yashin Prize for goalkeeper of the year six times.

FYODOR SMOLOV

Tall striker Fyodor Smolov is at the peak of his powers for club and country.

The 28-year-old spent the early years of his career with Dynamo Moscow but had several spells out on loan, with Feyenoord, Anzhi Makhachkala and Ural Yekaterinburg.

It was his move to Krasnodar in 2015 that really ignited his career, though. Since joining them his goals output has been phenomenal, and he was top goalscorer in the Russian league in 2015-16 and 2016-17.

He is in double figures of goals for his country, having made his international debut in 2012, and illustrated his quality by scoring twice against Spain in November.

YURI ZHIRKOV

One of the most experienced heads in the Russian team, the host nation will rely heavily on a player who has plenty of major tournament game-time behind him.

The left-sided midfielder, who can also fill in at left-back, has played for several of his country's biggest clubs including CSKA Moscow, Anzhi Makhachkala, Dynamo Moscow and Zenit St Petersburg, and also had a two-year spell with Chelsea.

His international career began way back in 2005 and has taken in a FIFA World Cup, UEFA European Championships and the FIFA Confederations Cup.

Nothing, however, will top playing in a home FIFA World Cup.

FIFA World Cup™ Record

1930	DNE	1958	QF	1978	DNQ	1998	DNQ
1934	DNE	1962	QF	1982	R2	2002	GS
1938	DNE	1966	4th	1986	16	2006	DNQ
1950	DNE	1970	QF	1990	GS	2010	DNQ
1954	DNE	1974	DNE	1994	GS	2014	GS

DNE = Did not enter, **DNQ** = Did not qualify, **W** = Withdrew, **R1** = Round 1, **R2** = Round 2, **GS** = Group Stages, **16** = Last 16, **QF** = Quarter-finals, **4th** = Fourth place, **3rd** = Third place, **RU** = Runners-up, **C** = Champions

Statistics up until February 2018

GROUP **A**
Russia
Saudi Arabia
Egypt
Uruguay

SAUDI ARABIA

Saudi Arabia, or the *Green Falcons* as they are sometimes known, come into the 2018 FIFA World Cup™ following a 12-year absence.

Their first experience at the world's greatest football tournament happened in 1994 and was the first of four consecutive FIFA World Cups™ they qualified for.

This first foray was also their most successful. Drawn in a group with the Netherlands, Belgium and Morocco, victories over the Belgians and Moroccans saw them progress to the round of 16 where they lost out to a strong Sweden side.

The next three occasions they qualified resulted in group-stage exits for the Saudis.

Their international tournament experience doesn't end there, however.

They took part in the first FIFA Confederations Cup in 1992 and finished as runners-up to Argentina, taking part in a further three editions of the competition.

They have also claimed three AFC Asia Cup titles in 1984, 1988 and 1996, coming second on three further occasions.

Dutchman Bert van Marwijk led the team through their qualifying campaign for the 2018 FIFA World Cup. He left his role in September 2017 but his replacement, Edgardo Bauza, only lasted five games.

Former Chile boss Juan Antonio Pizzi has now taken up the reins and he will be hoping to mastermind a strong showing in Russia.

The squad he has to choose from are almost entirely based with Saudi clubs so Pizzi will hope to pass on some of his knowledge of other footballing cultures to allow his players to prosper at the highest level.

"When our spirit comes to the fore, the Green Falcons are unstoppable."
— Fahad Al Muwallad

HOW THEY QUALIFIED

Saudi Arabia had to come through two group phases to claim their place at the 2018 FIFA World Cup.

The first group phase saw them go unbeaten over eight matches with United Arab Emirates, Palestine, Malaysia and Timor-Leste to top the standings, scoring 28 goals while only conceding four.

The top two in each six-team group in the next round would book their place in Russia and the Saudis did that by finishing second, a point behind Japan.

A tight group, also containing Australia, United Arab Emirates, Iraq and Thailand, ended with Saudi Arabia and Australia level on 19 points each, but the Saudis edged second place on goal difference.

The final group game proved crucial in their progress as they overcame group winners Japan 1-0 in Jeddah thanks to a goal from Fahad Al Muwallad.

It was then that the celebrations could begin and attention turned to Russia.

Russia
Saudi Arabia
Egypt
Uruguay

GROUP A

ALL-TIME TOP GOALSCORER	ALL-TIME MOST CAPS
MAJED ABDULLAH 71	MOHAMED AL-DEAYEA 178 

THE COACH

JUAN ANTONIO PIZZI

Juan Antonio Pizzi has only been in charge of the Saudi Arabia team for a few months but he will hope that is long enough to create a winning formula.

The Argentinian national started his career in his homeland but went on to play in Spain and ended up representing his new home in international football 22 times, scoring eight goals.

His career in management has seen him take charge of several clubs in South America and Spain but his most notable success came in leading Chile to *Copa América* glory in 2016, before he resigned following the Chileans' failure to reach the 2018 FIFA World Cup.

"We hope we can prepare well and compete against the best. Nowadays all the information is available and that is very important for coaches, so we're going to come up with the best plan we can."

HAT-TRICK OF HEROES

TAISIR AL JASSAM

With well over 100 caps, Taisir Al Jassam is one of the most experienced players in the Saudi squad.

Barring two loan spells, he has played his entire club career with Al-Ahli since 2004, winning several titles and having the honour of being named Saudi Arabia Footballer of the Year in 2012.

As an attacking midfielder he likes to show his skills and get on the scoresheet, and he managed six goals during his country's FIFA World Cup qualifying campaign.

He has also been a key part of the squad in three separate AFC Asia Cup campaigns.

MOHAMMED AL SAHLAWI

The chief goal-getter for Saudi Arabia is Mohammed Al Sahlawi.

The skilful striker, who will be 31 years old by the time the tournament begins, topped the goal charts in FIFA World Cup qualifying with 16 and will hope to take that form to Russia with him.

Since 2009 he has played his club football for Al-Nassr and averages a goal every other game.

In FIFA World Cup qualifying, Al Sahlawi hit two hat-tricks against Timor Leste in an eight-goal haul over both matches.

OSAMA HAWSAWI

Veteran defender Osama Hawsawi, 34, has played for the national team for over a decade, clocking up well over a century of caps.

Hawsawi has spent most of his career in Saudi club football, playing for Al-Wahda, Al-Ahli and having two spells with Al-Hilal, but in 2012 he became the only player from his country playing in Europe when he signed for Anderlecht.

Internationally, he was a part of the Saudi squad that finished second in the AFC Asian Cup in 2007 and also came runners-up in the Gulf Cup of Nations twice. He also had the distinction of scoring against Spain only a few months before the Spaniards became world champions in 2010.

FIFA World Cup™ Record

1930	DNE	1958	DNE	1978	DNQ	1998	GS
1934	DNE	1962	DNE	1982	DNQ	2002	GS
1938	DNE	1966	DNE	1986	DNQ	2006	GS
1950	DNE	1970	DNE	1990	DNQ	2010	DNQ
1954	DNE	1974	DNE	1994	16	2014	DNQ

DNE = Did not enter, **DNQ** = Did not qualify, **W** = Withdrew, **R1** = Round 1, **R2** = Round 2, **GS** = Group Stages, **16** = Last 16, **QF** = Quarter-finals, **4th** = Fourth place, **3rd** = Third place, **RU** = Runners-up, **C** = Champions

Statistics up until February 2018

GROUP A — Russia, Saudi Arabia, **Egypt**, Uruguay

EGYPT

One look at the wild, wild scenes in Cairo and beyond were all it took to understand exactly how much qualification for the 2018 FIFA World Cup Russia™ meant to the people of Egypt.

When Mo Salah slotted home a 95th-minute penalty against Congo to help Egypt to a 2-1 win in October last year, the country could finally celebrate returning to the top table of world football.

For much of the past decade or so, Egypt has been one of Africa's strongest sides but real success has eluded them due to political instability at home and also the Port Said disaster of 2012, which so devastated the country and its footballing followers.

However, Salah's brilliance and Egypt's first qualification for a FIFA World Cup™ since 1990 means those painful memories are just that; memories. Egypt are all about the here and now and are desperately keen to show the world what it has been missing in the 28-year hiatus from this tournament.

Their eagerness to shine in Russia will partly be down to the fact they missed out on the last two FIFA World Cups at the heartbreaking play-off stage and they also lost in the final of the AFC Africa Cup of Nations 2017 to Cameroon.

So much, therefore, of Egypt's recent history – footballing and otherwise – has been tinged with sadness but as those Cairo scenes proved, happier times are now on the horizon.

> "The fact that I still have a chance to play at the World Cup makes me even more motivated to continue playing to realise this dream."
>
> — Essam El-Hadary

HOW THEY QUALIFIED

Since 1990, qualifying campaigns for Egypt have been one long source of pain; especially ahead of the FIFA World Cups in 2010 and 2014 when they lost in qualifying play-off matches against Algeria and Ghana respectively.

The losses were felt with real pain by Egypt's fans who follow the national team with a passion and commitment that is truly outstanding. Yet those bad times are all over now because the *Pharaohs* made it this time around.

In Group E, Egypt had to fend off Uganda, Ghana and Congo and they did this with aplomb, winning four of their six matches to top the group with 13 points, four more than Uganda.

The penultimate game against Congo was the most crucial as Egypt still had their Russian destiny in their own hands and Salah was the difference, scoring both goals in a 2-1 win to send Egypt's players and fans crazy at the Borg El Arab Stadium.

Russia
Saudi Arabia
Egypt
Uruguay

GROUP **A**

FIFA WORLD CUP RUSSIA 2018

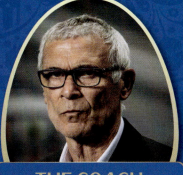

THE COACH

ALL-TIME TOP GOALSCORER
HOSSAM HASSAN
69

ALL-TIME MOST CAPS
AHMED HASSAN
184

HAT-TRICK OF HEROES

MOHAMED SALAH
Mo Salah is already a star at Anfield and he's only been there for one season.

Signed by Jürgen Klopp for Liverpool from AS Roma, Salah's brilliantly creative style and eye for goal means he is one of the Premier League's hottest properties.

Anfield has seen some truly wonderful footballers over the years and is rightly regarded as one of football's most famous cathedrals but very few Liverpool players can be said to have had the same immediate impact as Salah.

The current African Footballer of the Year is well on his way to being an all-time great.

HÉCTOR CÚPER
In March 2015, Héctor Cúper was announced as the new Egypt boss but his appointment was hardly greeted with wild acclaim. How times have changed.

After just one previous international management spell with Georgia, Cúper has settled in brilliantly as Egypt manager and masterminded their route to Russia.

The Cameroon loss last year in the AFC Africa Cup of Nations was a blow but Cúper has regrouped and re-energised his squad and is now hugely respected and admired in his adopted country.

Egypt's supporters place their footballing stars on a pedestal and if Cúper's men perform well in Russia, he will be forever adored in Egypt.

ESSAM EL-HADARY
When Egypt goalkeeper and captain Essam El-Hadary made his international debut way back in 1996, some of his current team-mates were not even born!

El-Hadary has had a truly remarkable career and won the AFC Africa Cup of Nations on four occasions with Egypt.

After initially retiring from international football in 2013, he changed his mind and returned to Egypt duty a year later – and how he must be thankful now that he did.

He will be the oldest ever player at a FIFA World Cup if his dream of appearing comes true. All the signs say that those dreams will indeed become reality.

"Football is a passion: if you don't have that, there's something missing. Football gives me life, oxygen; it always moves me, motivates me."

MOHAMED ELNENY
Arsenal's Mohamed Elneny has become a hugely important and influential player for Egypt. He is the kind of player who does the unfashionable midfield jobs – and he does them very well indeed.

To catch the eye of a managerial great like Arsène Wenger takes some doing but the former Basel star has superb ability and specialises in breaking up opposition attacks.

Like many people across the footballing spectrum who do the same kind of job as Elneny, he is one of Egypt's quieter heroes – but those he plays alongside know his worth.

FIFA World Cup™ Record

1930	DNE	1958	W	1978	DNQ	1998	DNQ
1934	GS	1962	W	1982	DNQ	2002	DNQ
1938	W	1966	W	1986	DNQ	2006	DNQ
1950	DNE	1970	DNE	1990	GS	2010	DNQ
1954	DNQ	1974	DNQ	1994	DNQ	2014	DNQ

DNE = Did not enter, **DNQ** = Did not qualify, **W** = Withdrew, **R1** = Round 1, **R2** = Round 2, **GS** = Group Stages, **16** = Last 16, **QF** = Quarter-finals, **4th** = Fourth place, **3rd** = Third place, **RU** = Runners-up, **C** = Champions

Statistics up until February 2018

GROUP A
- Russia
- Saudi Arabia
- Egypt
- **Uruguay**

URUGUAY

Winners in their first two attempts but failing to go beyond the semi-finals ever since, Uruguay have struggled to even qualify for a number of recent FIFA World Cup™ finals.

A memorable run to the last four in South Africa aside, the South Americans have flattered to deceive on the world stage despite their unparalleled successes in *Copa América* finals, and having included incredible strikers such as Luis Suárez, Edinson Cavani and Diego Forlán in their ranks.

La Celeste did make far easier work of their CONMEBOL qualification campaign this time around, ending as runners-up to Brazil – a country almost 50 times its size and with over 60 times its population.

Their previous four attempts finished with a play-off match, winning three and losing the other.

Long-serving manager Óscar Tabárez has a vastly-experienced squad at this disposal to choose from, with players based in both South America and in the top leagues across Europe being the core of his side for many years.

Spearheaded by Suárez and Cavani, a mixture of goals and guile back them up in midfield in the form of Cristian Rodríguez and Nicolás Lodeiro, with record appearance holder Maxi Pereira and captain Diego Godín the rocks in defence.

Their chances of reaching the knockout stages for the third FIFA World Cup finals in succession will rarely be more favourable, however, as they are the highest FIFA-ranked nation drawn in Group A. But with a potential tie against either Spain or Portugal in the round of 16 to follow, this settled side won't be taking anything for granted.

> "It will be great to take part and help out, I am really excited."
> — Luis Suárez

HOW THEY QUALIFIED

Uruguay will arrive in Russia after – compared to recent failures and play-off escapes – a relatively straightforward qualification campaign.

Skipper Diego Godín led by example in the opening matches by netting in each of Uruguay's first three group-stage victories before striker Edinson Cavani's scoring touch continued the encouraging qualification bid that was steadily gaining momentum. Beating both fellow qualification hopefuls Colombia and Chile 3-0 early on had Uruguay well on their way.

A late 2016/early 2017 dip in form threatened to spoil all their good work after seven wins in the first 11 matches had *La Celeste* well placed to progress. Three defeats on the bounce that included a heavy reverse to Brazil put a place in the automatic qualifying spots in doubt.

Victory over the chasing Paraguay last September though was a classic six-pointer that gave them the breathing space to eventually finish second in the group behind runaway leaders Brazil.

Russia
Saudi Arabia
Egypt
Uruguay

GROUP A

FIFA WORLD CUP RUSSIA 2018

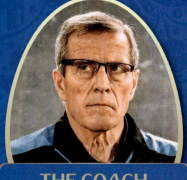

THE COACH

ÓSCAR TABÁREZ
Approaching 200 games in charge across 20 years and two spells in the role, the 2018 FIFA World Cup™ will be 71-year-old Óscar Tabárez's fourth finals as Uruguay coach.

The former defender and primary school teacher was central to Uruguay's change in fortunes on his reappointment in 2006 after the country failed to qualify for the finals for a third time in four attempts.

Establishing a 4-3-3 system right through the senior and youth levels of the national side, Tabárez's philosophy culminated in victory at the 2011 *Copa América* and a fourth-place finish at the 2010 FIFA World Cup™.

> "There are no easy matches at the World Cup, so I don't know why the people are celebrating our group as if we scored a goal in a match."

ALL-TIME TOP GOALSCORER
LUIS SUÁREZ
49

ALL-TIME MOST CAPS
MAXI PEREIRA
124

HAT-TRICK OF HEROES

EDINSON CAVANI
The outright top scorer in the South American qualifying rounds with ten goals, PSG forward Cavani is part of what is surely one of the most feared forward lines at the 2018 FIFA World Cup.

The 31-year-old comes to Russia having scored at least 25 club goals in each of the last eight seasons.

A powerful presence in attack, Cavani scored on his international bow back in 2008 and recently became one of a handful of players to earn a 100th cap for *La Celeste*.

His next aim then must be to compete with strike partner Luis Suárez for the title of Uruguay's all-time leading scorer.

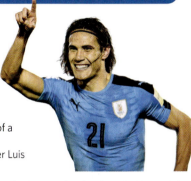

DIEGO GODÍN
A leader for club and country, Godín has enjoyed a decorated career that has brought domestic and European honours with Atlético Madrid – most famously the *La Liga* success in 2013/14 – as well as a *Copa América* crown, the captaincy and well over 100 caps for Uruguay.

Three of the central defender's eight international goals came in 2018 qualifying to kick-start their campaign, and he also scored in a 1-0 victory over Italy at the 2014 FIFA World Cup™ in Brazil that sent them through to the last 16.

The 32-year-old will be hoping his side can improve on their exit from the first knockout stage this time round.

LUIS SUÁREZ
A tenacious centre-forward of the highest order, more than 400 career goals speak for themselves and mark Luis Suárez out as the number-one threat Uruguay bring to Russia.

Now 31, the Barcelona striker is already in the top ten of the Catalan club's all-time leading goalscorers, and has held the record for his country since 2013.

Although his 2017/18 return has not reached the high standards set in previous seasons – at his peak he hit 59 in 53 games in 2015/16 – any defenders underestimating Suárez come the finals would be doing so at their peril.

FIFA World Cup™ Record

1930	C	1958	DNQ	1978	DNQ	1998	DNQ
1934	DNE	1962	GS	1982	DNQ	2002	GS
1938	DNE	1966	QF	1986	16	2006	DNQ
1950	C	1970	4th	1990	16	2010	4th
1954	4th	1974	GS	1994	DNQ	2014	16

DNE = Did not enter, **DNQ** = Did not qualify, **W** = Withdrew, **R1** = Round 1, **R2** = Round 2, **GS** = Group Stages, **16** = Last 16, **QF** = Quarter-finals, **4th** = Fourth place, **3rd** = Third place, **RU** = Runners-up, **C** = Champions

Statistics up until February 2018

PORTUGAL

SPAIN

MOROCCO

IR IRAN

FIFA WORLD CUP RUSSIA 2018

Group B Fixtures

15 JUNE
Morocco v. IR Iran
16:00
Saint Petersburg Stadium,
Saint Petersburg

15 JUNE
Portugal v. Spain
19:00
Fisht Stadium,
Sochi

20 JUNE
Portugal v. Morocco
13:00
Luzhniki Stadium,
Moscow

20 JUNE
IR Iran v. Spain
19:00
Kazan Arena,
Kazan

25 JUNE
IR Iran v. Portugal
19:00
Mordovia Arena,
Saransk

25 JUNE
Spain v. Morocco
19:00
Kaliningrad Stadium,
Kaliningrad

Kick-offs are UK time (UTC/GMT)

OFFICIAL 2018 FIFA WORLD CUP™ TOURNAMENT MAGAZINE 57

GROUP **B**
Portugal
Spain
Morocco
IR Iran

PORTUGAL

For many years, Portugal had a talented team that never quite delivered what their potential promised. In 2016, all of that changed.

Technically gifted with players that were coveted all around the world, it was a mystery that the Portuguese had so often failed to deliver in finals of major tournaments – or not even qualified for them at all.

That is why UEFA EURO 2016 was not only a wonderful triumph for Fernando Santos' men, it gave a team and a nation the belief and confidence that it could succeed against the world's best.

It also allowed one of the planet's greatest players to achieve a lifetime's ambition as Cristiano Ronaldo lifted the Henri Delaunay Trophy and claimed a major title with his country to add to the countless cups and individual honours he has won in his club career.

Until 2016, the best Portugal had managed was a selection of near-misses – particularly in the European Championships. They had reached the semi-finals three times and the quarter-finals twice, failing to qualify on eight occasions.

The FIFA World Cup™ has proven to be a tougher nut to crack.

With Eusébio scoring nine goals, the 1966 FIFA World Cup™ seemed to announce Portugal as a footballing force as they reached the semi-finals before losing out to England at Wembley.

However, they failed to qualify for seven out of the next eight FIFA World Cups and, a fourth-place finish in 2006 aside, the best they have managed is a place in the last 16.

Maybe now is Portugal's time to conquer the world.

> "Just like we did at the Euros, we are going to try to win the World Cup as well."
> — Bernardo Silva

HOW THEY QUALIFIED

It's not how you start the race that counts; it's how you finish it.

Portugal spent the majority of their campaign trailing Switzerland in European qualifying Group B as both sides set a ferocious pace at the top of Europe's tightest group.

With Hungary, Faroe Islands, Latvia and Andorra never likely to challenge at the top, Switzerland's 2-0 win over the Portuguese in the first match was the difference between the sides until they met again in the final round of group games.

Portugal knew they had to win and on home turf, in front of a packed Estádio da Luz in Lisbon, they produced the goods as an own goal from Johan Djourou and a further strike from André Silva sealed a 2-0 win and progress to the 2018 FIFA World Cup™.

And there was no surprise to see Cristiano Ronaldo top-score for Portugal during the qualifying campaign, hitting 15 goals – only one fewer than Poland's prolific Robert Lewandowski.

Portugal
Spain
Morocco
IR Iran

GROUP B

FIFA WORLD CUP RUSSIA 2018

ALL-TIME TOP GOALSCORER
CRISTIANO RONALDO
79

ALL-TIME MOST CAPS
CRISTIANO RONALDO
147

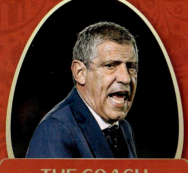

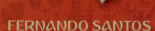
THE COACH

FERNANDO SANTOS

Fernando Santos was made for Portugal and Portugal was made for Fernando Santos.

The 63-year-old Portuguese will forever be a hero in his country of birth after leading Portugal to their first-ever major trophy, when they won the UEFA European Championships in 2016.

His journey to his job as national team coach was a long one, taking in numerous clubs in Portugal and Greece. Along the way, he won five major titles with Porto and cut his teeth as an international manager with Greece from 2010-14.

He will hope his calm influence will inspire Portugal to another spectacular summer.

"There is a perfect symbiosis between coach and player. I always believe in my players. It is not easy to have 25 players with this mindset and it creates a fantastic environment. I believe in our work."

HAT-TRICK OF HEROES

BRUNO ALVES

Classy, tough-tackling defender Bruno Alves has been a regular part of the Portuguese line-up for over a decade.

Closing in on a century of appearances for his country, he has been recognised as one of Europe's top defenders, especially during his trophy-laden spell with Porto.

He has also won honours with Zenit St Petersburg and Fenerbahçe and has been playing his club football in Scotland with Rangers.

The bonus with Alves is that he knows where the net is. He has a goal total in double figures for his country and will look to add to that in Russia.

JOÃO MOUTINHO

Among the plethora of experienced professionals who have formed the backbone of the Portugal team for the past decade is João Moutinho.

The busy midfielder has over 100 caps for his country and is one of the first names on the team sheet.

Most of his club career has been played in his homeland, winning a dozen trophies for Porto and Sporting, winning Player of the Year for the former in 2013.

These days he's part of an exciting Monaco team and won *Ligue 1* with them in 2017.

Aged 31, there's plenty more gas in the tank.

CRISTIANO RONALDO

Quite simply, Cristiano Ronaldo is one of the best players ever to grace a football pitch and he would walk into any team on the planet.

While his ability is outstanding, it's his goal record that marks him out as unique.

He is Real Madrid's top goalscorer of all time, he is Portugal's top goalscorer of all time, and he has over 600 goals for club and country. He is also the only player ever to have scored 30 goals or more in six consecutive *La Liga* seasons.

About the only thing he hasn't done in his career is win the FIFA World Cup™...

FIFA World Cup™ Record

1930	DNE	1958	DNQ	1978	DNQ	1998	DNQ
1934	DNQ	1962	DNQ	1982	DNQ	2002	GS
1938	DNQ	1966	3rd	1986	GS	2006	4th
1950	DNQ	1970	DNQ	1990	DNQ	2010	16
1954	DNQ	1974	DNQ	1994	DNQ	2014	GS

DNE = Did not enter, **DNQ** = Did not qualify, **W** = Withdrew, **R1** = Round 1, **R2** = Round 2, **GS** = Group Stages, **16** = Last 16, **QF** = Quarter-finals, **4th** = Fourth place, **3rd** = Third place, **RU** = Runners-up, **C** = Champions

Statistics up until February 2018

GROUP B
Portugal
Spain
Morocco
IR Iran

SPAIN

For a long, long time, it seemed that Spain would be destined to be an acclaimed national side that never quite did enough to win a FIFA World Cup™. However, that all changed eight years ago.

Under legendary manager Vicente Del Bosque, Spain finally removed the shackles of history – their best previous finish had been fourth spot in 1950 – and they lifted the official trophy in South Africa in 2010.

Spain is one of the most football-mad countries on Earth and the success of Del Bosque's side led to huge celebrations across the country.

After also winning UEFA EURO 2008 and UEFA EURO 2012, it was clear that Spain were the greatest footballing side on the planet but any hopes of defending their FIFA World Cup crown were extinguished in Brazil four years ago after losses in their opening two matches against the Netherlands and Chile.

In the time since then – especially after another disappointing tournament at UEFA EURO 2016 – a lot has changed in Spain's squad and players like Koke, Álvaro Morata, Thiago Alcântara and Isco have stepped up to the plate for La Roja in recent times.

Del Bosque left after UEFA EURO 2016 for a well-deserved retirement and a place in the pantheon of footballing greats.

The current Spain team are still developing and finding a new identity under Julen Lopetegui and he has proven a more than worthy replacement as he looks to take Spain back to the summit of international sport.

> "We know it's going to be very difficult to match the achievements of the past. The generation that's coming through has big dreams, though."
>
> — Jorge 'Koke' Resurrección

HOW THEY QUALIFIED

Spain have one of the richest pedigrees imaginable when it comes to qualifying for the FIFA World Cup.

They are now unbeaten in FIFA World Cup qualifying matches since losing to Denmark on 31 March 1993. That is a run of 63 unbeaten matches with 50 wins and 13 draws.

In Group G, they booked their place at the 2018 FIFA World Cup™ by beating Italy to top spot in the group and a victory over Albania in October last year ensured they qualified with a match to spare.

A 3-0 win over Italy in September 2017 proved crucial as two goals from Isco and one from Álvaro Morata sealed victory.

Spain scored 36 goals in their qualifying campaign and conceded just three goals in ten matches, a quite incredible feat.

The rest of the footballing world will already have been fearing Spain anyway but the manner in which they qualified for Russia should ensure Spain go into the tournament as one of the favourites.

Portugal
Spain
Morocco
IR Iran

GROUP **B**

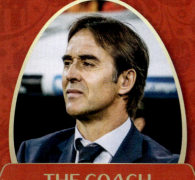

THE COACH

JULEN LOPETEGUI

Replacing Vicente Del Bosque would be a daunting task for any individual but Julen Lopetegui deserves credit for the way he has stepped out of Del Bosque's shadow.

One of his strengths is that he knows a lot of his players from his time in charge of Spain's youth teams.

Lopetegui is a widely respected coach who loves to get out on the training ground and he has also shown plenty of tactical prowess while in charge of Spain. This was particularly evident in the way he masterminded a 3-0 victory over Italy in the 2018 FIFA World Cup qualifier in September last year which scuppered Italy's hopes of winning Group G.

"I've been lucky to have players that have shown so much commitment and their impeccable attitude has helped a lot. We are delighted and proud of what we have achieved because it's very important for Spain."

ALL-TIME TOP GOALSCORER
DAVID VILLA
59

ALL-TIME MOST CAPS
IKER CASILLAS
167

HAT-TRICK OF HEROES

ISCO

Isco is the latest talented midfield playmaker to emerge from the Spanish conveyor belt and the Real Madrid star is maturing into one of Spain's biggest threats.

His performance against Italy in their 3-0 qualifying win was superb and underlines his ability when he gets time on the ball.

Isco's set-piece delivery is fantastic and he can be deadly with free-kicks around the penalty area.

He is sure to cause plenty of sleepless nights for defenders in Russia and he has a golden opportunity at the 2018 FIFA World Cup to show Spain's fans – and the watching world – that he can perform heroics at the very highest level and on a consistent basis.

SERGIO RAMOS

Sergio Ramos is the kind of defender and leader who divides opinion but his leadership of both his national side and Real Madrid proves how valuable he is to Spain.

Although not particularly tall, the central defender is an outstanding reader of the game, he tackles hard and his commitment to Spain's cause is absolute.

He broke his nose in the Madrid derby last November but immediately stated he would be back as soon as possible, perfectly underlining his bravery and no-nonsense approach.

Every successful side needs a strong spine and a strong central defence and Ramos is the ideal man for the job.

DAVID SILVA

David Silva is, quite simply, a footballing magician.

Although small in stature, he has thrived in the physical world of the Premier League and his genius on the ball for Manchester City is well known.

In a side crammed with world-class players at City, Silva still manages to stand out and he is the kind of wizard who appears to have all the time in the world when on the ball.

Few players in the game can launch an attack as quickly or as effectively as Silva and he somehow appears to be getting better with age.

If he gets the ball often enough, anything can happen.

FIFA World Cup™ Record

Year	Result	Year	Result	Year	Result	Year	Result
1930	DNE	1958	DNQ	1978	GS	1998	GS
1934	QF	1962	GS	1982	16	2002	QF
1938	W	1966	GS	1986	QF	2006	16
1950	4th	1970	DNQ	1990	16	2010	C
1954	DNQ	1974	DNQ	1994	QF	2014	GS

DNE = Did not enter, **DNQ** = Did not qualify, **W** = Withdrew, **R1** = Round 1, **R2** = Round 2, **GS** = Group Stages, **16** = Last 16, **QF** = Quarter-finals, **4th** = Fourth place, **3rd** = Third place, **RU** = Runners-up, **C** = Champions

Statistics up until February 2018

GROUP **B**
Portugal
Spain
Morocco
IR Iran

MOROCCO

For Morocco, the long wait is now over.

For 20 years, fans of the *Atlas Lions* have seen FIFA World Cups™ come and go and watched the party go on without them.

It is two decades since they last played on the biggest stage and the country's celebrations when they qualified showed just how much it meant to be back competing against the world's best.

Morocco's presence at the 2018 FIFA World Cup Russia™ is no accident either as they have a squad capable of really making an impact at the highest level.

Stars such as Mehdi Benatia, Nabil Dirar, Nordin Amrabat, Khalid Boutaïb and Younès Belhanda all represent the selfless and attacking instinct which saw Morocco do so well in qualifying.

Morocco's style of play is based around relentless physicality, supreme fitness and a superb team spirit and they will need to harness all of those in Russia if they want to become the first African team since Ghana at the 2010 FIFA World Cup™ to reach the quarter-finals.

Morocco's best performance at a FIFA World Cup came in 1986 when they reached the last 16 in Mexico after topping a group that contained England, Poland and Portugal.

Whatever happens in Russia, the very presence of Morocco and their colourful fans will certainly create plenty of talking points, and with manager Hervé Renard insisting his side are there to compete on level terms, Morocco could well provide a shock or two as the tournament progresses.

> "It's been 20 years... 20 years is too much. Thanks God, we are going to take our children and families to Russia. But we are not going there for tourism."
>
> — *Mehdi Benatia*

HOW THEY QUALIFIED

Morocco joined Tunisia, Nigeria, Egypt and Senegal as Africa's representatives at the 2018 FIFA World Cup with a brilliant 2-0 victory away at Côte d'Ivoire.

It was a winner-takes-all scenario in Abidjan as the winner of the match would qualify for Russia, but it was Morocco who held their nerve for longer as goals from Nabil Dirar and captain Mehdi Benatia ensured Morocco finished at the top of Africa's Group C.

In earlier qualifying matches, Morocco were held to goalless draws against Gabon and Côte d'Ivoire early on but they then showed their attacking spirit with a 6-0 victory over Mali and a 3-0 win over Gabon, setting up their mouth-watering last match against Côte d'Ivoire.

With 11 goals scored in Group C, Morocco topped the scoring charts and also did not concede in any of their six encounters, a remarkable feat at any level of football.

Defending like that will mean the *Atlas Lions* will be a tough nut to crack for even the world's best.

Portugal
Spain
Morocco
IR Iran

GROUP B

FIFA WORLD CUP RUSSIA 2018

THE COACH

HERVÉ RENARD

Winning the CAF Africa Cup of Nations with one country is hard enough, but managing to do it with two is even more difficult, yet that is what Hervé Renard has already managed in his career.

The Frenchman won it with Zambia in 2012 and then Côte d'Ivoire in 2015 to become the first man to do so. His career has seen him manage in China, England and France, and he has also been in charge at Angola.

His straightforward approach and animated touchline behaviour ensure Renard is an interesting individual and he clearly has the full attention and admiration of the Moroccan dressing room.

"I am delighted for all the Moroccan fans who have encouraged their national team. We are proud of the Moroccan shirt, proud that the Moroccan flag returns to the World Cup. This is the fifth qualification so Morocco is not a small football country."

ALL-TIME TOP GOALSCORER
AHMED FARAS
42

ALL-TIME MOST CAPS
NOUREDDINE NAYBET
115

HAT-TRICK OF HEROES

MEHDI BENATIA

Mehdi Benatia plays for Juventus in *Serie A* and is one of the defensive linchpins of the Moroccan side.

With impressive clubs like Marseille, Roma and Bayern Munich on his CV, it is clear we are talking about a top-class operator.

By the time the 2018 FIFA World Cup Russia starts, he will be 31 so knows this could be his last opportunity to show the world what he is capable of.

Supremely committed and capable of causing goalscoring trouble himself from set-pieces, Benatia will do whatever it takes to help Morocco thrive in Russia.

NORDIN AMRABAT

Nordin Amrabat is a pacy winger who has spent last season playing for Leganés in Spain, and although he was born in the Netherlands, he pledged sporting allegiance to Morocco in 2009.

He made his international debut in November 2011 and in his second game for Morocco he scored his first goal – against Cameroon.

His career has taken him to big clubs like PSV Eindhoven, Galatasaray and Malàga and also seen him ply his trade in the Premier League with Watford.

He has spoken previously about how qualifying for the 2018 FIFA World Cup Russia would be "a dream come true." His dreams are about to become a wonderful reality.

KHALID BOUTAÏB

Khalid Boutaïb only made his international debut in 2016 but he has not looked back and the goalscorer is a very dangerous man with the ball at his feet.

At 190cm tall, there is also an aerial threat from the man born in France to parents of Moroccan descent.

A latecomer on the international stage, he only made his debut for Morocco once he had turned 29.

He scored a hat-trick in the 3-0 qualifying win over Gabon to underline how talented he is and he is more than ready to try and live up to the expectations now on his shoulders.

FIFA World Cup™ Record

1930	DNE	1958	DNE	1978	DNQ	1998	GS
1934	DNE	1962	DNQ	1982	DNQ	2002	DNQ
1938	DNE	1966	W	1986	16	2006	DNQ
1950	DNE	1970	GS	1990	DNQ	2010	DNQ
1954	DNE	1974	DNQ	1994	GS	2014	DNQ

DNE = Did not enter, **DNQ** = Did not qualify, **W** = Withdrew, **R1** = Round 1, **R2** = Round 2, **GS** = Group Stages, **16** = Last 16, **QF** = Quarter-finals, **4th** = Fourth place, **3rd** = Third place, **RU** = Runners-up, **C** = Champions

Statistics up until February 2018

GROUP **B**
Portugal
Spain
Morocco
IR Iran

IR IRAN

This is IR Iran's fifth appearance at a FIFA World Cup™ event and all the omens suggest this could be their best-ever tournament.

After previously taking part in the 1978, 1998, 2006 and 2014 editions, IR Iran's appearance in Russia is their first back-to-back presence and manager Carlos Queiroz has forged a team that will create some major problems for their opponents.

During their brilliant qualifying campaign, overseen by a manager in Queiroz who is as experienced, knowledgeable and positive as it gets, IR Iran kept 12 consecutive clean sheets.

That is a remarkable statistic and underlines their strength in defence.

However, to suggest they put all 11 men behind the ball would be an incorrect assessment of Queiroz's tactics and of the type of play demanded by IR Iran's fanatical supporters.

Players like Sardar Azmoun, Ramin Rezaeian, and Mehdi Taremi are wonderfully gifted footballers and IR Iran have a brilliant team spirit and desire to win, which they will look to capitalise on as the tournament progresses.

Group B is a stunningly difficult group to compete in, and predict, as Spain, Portugal and Morocco all have some superb strengths of their own and it is clear that Spain and Portugal are the heavy favourites to progress.

Yet FIFA World Cup™ tournaments are all about upsets, surprises and amazing moments of footballing skill and IR Iran could well be one of the most talked-about countries involved in Russia if they can continue their brilliant recent form and harness the knowledge, advice and expertise of their hugely respected manager.

> "When I met them for the first time I saw so many talented players. I immediately felt like part of a big family."
> — Saman Ghoddos

HOW THEY QUALIFIED

Some teams stumbled and staggered on their way to the 2018 FIFA World Cup™ in Russia – but IR Iran were not one of them.

In fact, they were the second team to qualify for the tournament behind Brazil (Russia having already qualified as hosts of course) and emulating Brazil at anything involving football is no mean feat.

In Group A of Asia's final round of qualifying, IR Iran were simply too good for their opponents and their presence in Russia was confirmed as far back as June 2017.

On a passionate night at the Azadi Stadium in Tehran – truly one of world football's most exciting and intimidating arenas – IR Iran overcame Uzbekistan 2-0 thanks to goals from Sardar Azmoun and Mehdi Taremi.

Overall, Queiroz's side played 18 matches in qualifying and lost none of them. That is a truly remarkable feat at any level of football, especially international matches where FIFA World Cup™ spots and national pride are at stake.

Portugal
Spain
Morocco
IR Iran

GROUP **B**

FIFA WORLD CUP RUSSIA 2018

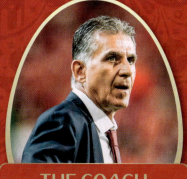

THE COACH

CARLOS QUEIROZ

Some people will remember Carlos Queiroz best for his unflappable nature as Sir Alex Ferguson's assistant manager at Manchester United from 2004-2008, but he has done enough himself to deserve merit for his own achievements.

Queiroz was appointed IR Iran's manager in 2011 and is the nation's longest-serving manager and something of a national hero after guiding them to two FIFA World Cup tournaments.

His impressive CV includes two spells as Portugal manager, short stints in charge of South Africa and the United Arab Emirates, plus club management with Sporting and Real Madrid.

"From the players' point of view, I'm sure they are very excited to play against Portugal and Spain and also Morocco, because it's a unique and rare opportunity for Iranian players to play against such great players and such great teams."

ALL-TIME TOP GOALSCORER
ALI DAEI
109

ALL-TIME MOST CAPS
JAVED NEKOUNAM
151

HAT-TRICK OF HEROES

SARDAR AZMOUN

Sardar Azmoun currently plays his domestic football at Rubin Kazan after previous spells at Rostov and Sepahan.

Aged just 23, the forward is a powerful striker who loves to run in behind defenders and punish opposition players if they give him too much room.

He is already highly-placed on IR Iran's all-time goalscoring list and has a remarkable goals-to-games ratio. He will never have a better opportunity to show he belongs on the highest stage than the 2018 FIFA World Cup and his willingness to work hard for IR Iran is sure to get him spotted and respected around the globe.

REZA GHOOCHANNEJHAD

Reza Ghoochannejhad has played in various locations around the world and the 30-year-old has been in constant demand for over a decade; proof indeed of his goalscoring proficiency and his wily, intelligent style of play.

He originally represented Netherlands youth teams before declaring allegiance for IR Iran in 2012 – and that was a move that has brilliantly paid off for all parties.

Ghoochannejhad has FIFA World Cup experience already, courtesy of his presence at the 2014 edition, and he will be looked to for goals, guidance and glory in Russia.

MEHDI TAREMI

Mehdi Taremi is one of the most in-demand Iranian players on the planet and rightly so.

At 25, he is coming into his own as a professional footballer and, like his older brother Mohammad, he is a fine player who is equally comfortable as a striker or as an attacking midfielder.

Taremi is notable for his selfless style and he appears to be comfortable with the ball at his feet or in the air.

Never content to let the match drift, Taremi will happily go looking for the ball and for goalscoring opportunities and he is never far away from the action.

FIFA World Cup™ Record

1930	DNE	1958	DNE	1978	GS	1998	GS
1934	DNE	1962	DNE	1982	W	2002	DNQ
1938	DNE	1966	DNE	1986	DNE	2006	GS
1950	DNE	1970	DNE	1990	DNQ	2010	DNQ
1954	DNE	1974	DNQ	1994	DNQ	2014	GS

DNE = Did not enter, **DNQ** = Did not qualify, **W** = Withdrew, **R1** = Round 1, **R2** = Round 2, **GS** = Group Stages, **16** = Last 16, **QF** = Quarter-finals, **4th** = Fourth place, **3rd** = Third place, **RU** = Runners-up, **C** = Champions

Statistics up until February 2018

Defence of the crown

Four years after winning the FIFA World Cup™ on home soil, Italy proved they could travel abroad and still be as successful in 1938. They didn't have to travel too far though as a fruitful campaign in France culminated in a 4-2 victory over Hungary in the final, having knocked the hosts out in the quarter-finals. Here, coach Vittorio Pozzo proudly holds aloft the Jules Rimet Trophy at the Stade Olympique de Colombes in Paris.

FRANCE

AUSTRALIA

PERU

DENMARK

FIFA WORLD CUP RUSSIA 2018

Group C Fixtures

16 JUNE
France v. Australia
11:00
Kazan Arena,
Kazan

16 JUNE
Peru v. Denmark
17:00
Mordovia Arena,
Saransk

21 JUNE
Denmark v. Australia
13:00
Samara Arena,
Samara

21 JUNE
France v. Peru
16:00
Ekaterinburg Arena,
Ekaterinburg

26 JUNE
Australia v. Peru
15:00
Fisht Stadium,
Sochi

26 JUNE
Denmark v. France
15:00
Luzhniki Stadium,
Moscow

Kick-offs are UK time (UTC/GMT)

GROUP **C** — France / Australia / Peru / Denmark

FRANCE

France might not arrive in Russia as the favourites for 2018 FIFA World Cup™ glory but nobody should write off their chances. After all, they have form for stunning the footballing world.

In the final of the 1998 FIFA World Cup™ on their home soil in Paris, Brazil were the huge favourites to lift the trophy as they were led by the brilliance of Ronaldo. However, a Zinédine Zidane-inspired French side shocked everybody – and perhaps even themselves – when they won the final 3-0 on a quite wonderful and captivating July evening in the City of Light.

Since then, France's FIFA World Cup™ form has not been quite so impressive.

A run to the final of the 2006 FIFA World Cup™ apart, France were knocked out at the group stage in both 2002 and 2010 before reaching the quarter-final in Brazil four years ago. All that is now ancient history as Didier Deschamps and his wonderfully exciting squad get ready to travel to Russia.

The depth of the French squad is staggering, with the likes of Paul Pogba, Antoine Griezmann, Kylian Mbappé and Olivier Giroud offering plenty of attacking options.

France will travel east as dark horses but after what happened 20 years ago, only a fool would write them off.

What can be guaranteed is that Deschamps' men will be very fit, well-drilled and eager to get forward at every opportunity. And when you combine those qualities, absolutely anything can happen.

> *"After the World Cup it will be the right time to make room for the youngsters. I have six months left in the French team to take as many memories, as my wife would say."*
>
> — Laurent Koscielny

HOW THEY QUALIFIED

France qualified for their fifth successive FIFA World Cup but it was not always easy going in Group A.

Sweden and the Netherlands were both alongside France in the group while Bulgaria, Luxembourg and Belarus also posed their own dangers.

In their ten qualifying matches, France won seven, drew two and lost just one but they did not qualify outright as group winners until their tenth and final encounter, a 2-1 victory over Belarus at the Stade de France in October last year.

Goals from Antoine Griezmann and Olivier Giroud made all the difference and although Anton Saroka pulled one back for Belarus just before half-time, France remained strong after the interval to hold onto their lead and book their trip to Russia.

Both Sweden and the Netherlands scored more goals in the qualifying campaign but nobody could match France's defensive prowess as they conceded just six times.

France	GROUP
Australia	C
Peru	
Denmark	

FIFA WORLD CUP RUSSIA 2018

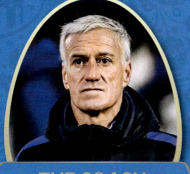

THE COACH

ALL-TIME TOP GOALSCORER
THIERRY HENRY
51

ALL-TIME MOST CAPS
LILIAN THURAM
142

HAT-TRICK OF HEROES

PAUL POGBA
Paul Pogba joined Manchester United in a world-record transfer move in August 2016 and having taken a while to settle, he is now one of the standout performers at Old Trafford.

The same can be said for him in a France shirt as well. The midfielder is a natural athlete, he is quick and strong and he can do everything you ask of him.

Equally adept defending or launching attacks, Pogba is a mainstay of France's set-up and can only get better in the years to come, especially if he continues to be such an important player at Manchester United.

HUGO LLORIS
Hugo Lloris has matured into one of the Premier League's finest goalkeepers in recent seasons.

Every successful team needs somebody between the posts who is first-class and Tottenham Hotspur are fortunate enough to call upon Lloris when they need to defend.

Lloris is a wonderful reader of the play, he is quick off his line, confident when collecting crosses and is probably the best shot-stopper in the English game.

Tottenham regularly have to fend off interest from other clubs keen on his services but Lloris gives his back four plenty of confidence and will be crucial to any French success.

ANTOINE GRIEZMANN
Antoine Griezmann made his France debut in 2014 and has already played over 50 times for his country, a sure sign of his worth to *Les Bleus*.

The striker is lethal in front of goal, he was the player of the tournament and top scorer at UEFA EURO 2016, and at just 26 he has a huge and successful future ahead of him.

When he gets the ball, opposition defenders start to get nervous, and rightly so.

Although he is not the biggest of players, Griezmann's intelligence, hard running and ability to out-think defenders means he is a thorn in the opposition's side.

DIDIER DESCHAMPS
Didier Deschamps will go down in French footballing history as the captain who lifted the FIFA World Cup Trophy after their glorious victory over Brazil in 1998.

He was an outstanding player in his day and he has worked hard to transfer his winning mindset across into his managerial career.

Deschamps has a plethora of impressive players to call on and he has been in charge since 2012, in which time France have made a marked improvement.

Deschamps is a man who demands total commitment from his men and they certainly look up to him, courtesy of his own brilliance in a French shirt during his playing days.

> "I am obviously very happy for the players because they deserve it. We're happy, although I know it's logical and normal given the quality of the players I have."

FIFA World Cup™ Record

1930	GS	1958	3rd	1978	GS	1998	C
1934	GS	1962	DNQ	1982	4th	2002	GS
1938	QF	1966	GS	1986	3rd	2006	RU
1950	W	1970	DNQ	1990	DNQ	2010	GS
1954	GS	1974	DNQ	1994	DNQ	2014	QF

DNE = Did not enter, **DNQ** = Did not qualify, **W** = Withdrew, **R1** = Round 1, **R2** = Round 2, **GS** = Group Stages, **16** = Last 16, **QF** = Quarter-finals, **4th** = Fourth place, **3rd** = Third place, **RU** = Runners-up, **C** = Champions

Statistics up until February 2018

GROUP C
France
Australia
Peru
Denmark

AUSTRALIA

Australia's journey in FIFA World Cups™ has never been a smooth ride but they will be desperately keen to change all that in Russia.

Australia did not enter the first seven FIFA World Cup tournaments as cricket, Australian Rules football and rugby league remained the country's sporting priorities.

However, over the decades, football has become an increasingly important and popular sport Down Under, and that has been reflected by the *Socceroos'* continued evolution into one of Asia's strongest nations.

Australia first qualified for a FIFA World Cup in 1974 but it would then be a huge 32-year wait before they would return to German soil for a second attempt, going out in the round of 16 in 2006 after demonstrating those typical Australian sporting strengths of tenacity and great fitness throughout a thrilling tournament.

Group-stage exits in 2010 and 2014 have done little to dampen the fervour around the national side nor the Australian public's desire to see their national team compete hard against some of football's more traditional super powers.

Certain aspects of an Australian football team can be taken for granted, such as a brilliant team spirit, a real, deep pride in representing their country and a willingness to fight hard for 90 minutes – and sometimes beyond – to help Australia to a win.

Make no mistake, this may only be Australia's fifth appearance at a FIFA World Cup but no squad in Russia will be more determined to prove they belong at football's top table.

> "I'm delighted to go to another World Cup. The captain's armband is a great honour. I try to be an example for my teammates."
>
> — Mile Jedinak —

HOW THEY QUALIFIED

Australia left it late to qualify for the 2018 FIFA World Cup Russia™ as they were the 31st team out of 32 to book their place at the tournament.

They did so by beating Honduras 3-1 in November 2017 in their intercontinental play-off after finishing qualifying as Asia's best third-placed side following a play-off with Syria.

The Honduras match was a nervy encounter early on in the ANZ Stadium in Sydney but finally swung in the *Socceroos'* favour when Mile Jedinak scored a second-half hat-trick to secure their place.

The sense of relief was palpable – as was the sense of delight that they would again be featuring in world football's premium tournament.

Ange Postecoglou, the manager who steered them through the World Cup qualification campaign, quit shortly afterwards but the *Socceroos* were in no mood to let that spoil their celebrations.

France
Australia
Peru
Denmark

GROUP C

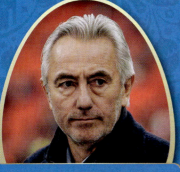

THE COACH

BERT VAN MARWIJK

When Ange Postecoglou stepped down as Australia coach after achieving FIFA World Cup qualification, Football Federation Australia (FFA) wanted a man of significant international football knowledge to take over – and that is exactly what they got.

The FFA took their time before concluding that former Netherlands and Saudi Arabia coach Bert van Marwijk would be their man.

Not only did Dutchman Van Marwijk lead his own country to the 2010 FIFA World Cup final, he also helped Saudi Arabia finish above the *Socceroos* to qualify for Russia, simultaneously proving his quality and gathering lots of knowledge of the team he now takes over.

> "I know a lot about the players and how the team has been playing after coaching against them for the two World Cup qualifiers, in 2016 and in June last year. I have also been impressed by the national team setup."

ALL-TIME TOP GOALSCORER
TIM CAHILL
50

ALL-TIME MOST CAPS
MARK SCHWARZER
109

HAT-TRICK OF HEROES

MILE JEDINAK

Mile Jedinak put in a real captain's performance in the crucial play-off against Honduras and he has become a fantastic *Socceroos* leader in recent years.

He wore the skipper's armband at the 2014 FIFA World Cup Brazil™ and also lifted the Asian Cup trophy as captain in 2015.

Australia will hope his impressive form – and leadership – will give them a boost in Russia.

Jedinak is a special kind of player who has ensured that the *Socceroos* dressing room is united behind him, and he sets the example for his loyal team-mates by always leading from the front.

TIM CAHILL

Tim Cahill is arguably the finest Australian footballer of all time.

After impressing for so long in the Premier League with Everton, he is held in similar awe by his national side.

He has scored at three FIFA World Cups – one of a select band who can claim that accolade – and his knack for a goal and his ability to be in the right place at the right time remains astonishing.

Cahill is not the tallest player but he is a wonderful header of the ball, and he is aggressive and committed to Australia's cause. No player has ever given more for his national team.

TOMAS ROGIC

Tomas Rogic is a legend in Scotland and he can become a legend in Australia too.

You do not become part of Celtic's incredible squad without being a fine player and the midfielder has become one of Australia's most consistent performers since making his international debut in 2012.

Rogic is one of the *Socceroos'* leading playmakers and he has carried his brilliant form for Celtic over the past few seasons into his performances for his country.

Rogic may not be the first name on everybody's lips when discussing who is shining in European football the most at the moment, but this tournament is his opportunity to change that for good.

FIFA World Cup™ Record

1930	DNE	1958	DNE	1978	DNQ	1998	DNQ
1934	DNE	1962	DNE	1982	DNQ	2002	DNQ
1938	DNE	1966	DNQ	1986	DNQ	2006	16
1950	DNE	1970	DNQ	1990	DNQ	2010	GS
1954	DNE	1974	GS	1994	DNQ	2014	GS

DNE = Did not enter, **DNQ** = Did not qualify, **W** = Withdrew, **R1** = Round 1, **R2** = Round 2, **GS** = Group Stages, **16** = Last 16, **QF** = Quarter-finals, **4th** = Fourth place, **3rd** = Third place, **RU** = Runners-up, **C** = Champions

Statistics up until February 2018

GROUP **C**
France
Australia
Peru
Denmark

PERU

It has been a long wait for fans of the Peru national team, but after a 36-year gap *La Blanquirroja* are back at a FIFA World Cup™.

The Peruvians are known for their slick passing, love of attacking and high technical quality, yet they have struggled in recent years to hit the heights.

The last time they qualified for a FIFA World Cup™ was in 1982 when two draws in their three games wasn't enough to see them progress beyond round one.

That was the third time in four FIFA World Cups that Peru made it to the party and the 1970s were a particularly strong time for the country with players like Hugo Sotil, Teófilo Cubillas and Héctor Chumpitaz leading the way.

That was also the decade when Peru won one of their two *Copa América* titles, with Sotil getting the only goal in the final against Colombia.

Before that you have to go back to 1939 to find the last time Peru won major silverware, when they landed the *Copa América* for the first time.

The 1930s was another decade when Peru were enjoying a purple patch as they took part in the first FIFA World Cup in 1930 in Uruguay, but they failed to make it beyond round one.

Peru do hold a unique piece of FIFA World Cup history as they won the inaugural FIFA Fair Play Trophy, awarded at the 1970 tournament, having been the only team not to receive any yellow or red cards during the competition.

> "It's a child's dream. It's a big emotion, beyond making history. We have not broken this bad streak for so long."
>
> — Christian Cueva

HOW THEY QUALIFIED

With only one win from their opening six group qualifying games, a place at the 2018 FIFA World Cup™ seemed a long way away. So the fact Peru came through the difficult South American group to ultimately qualify demonstrates the belief and ability they have in their squad.

They finished the qualifiers really strongly, winning three and drawing three of their final six games, including a 2-1 win over a very talented Uruguay team and a vital point away at Argentina in the penultimate game.

They finished the group in fifth place, which meant a play-off against a dangerous New Zealand side.

A 0-0 draw in the first leg left everything up for grabs in the return match in Lima and Peru made the most of an opportunity they were determined not to let slip by.

Goals from Jefferson Farfán and Christian Ramos did the job and made sure the Peruvians became the fifth South American nation to make it to Russia.

France
Australia
Peru
Denmark

GROUP C

FIFA WORLD CUP RUSSIA 2018

THE COACH

RICARDO GARECA
Known as *El Tigre* (the tiger), Ricardo Gareca's tenacious attitude clearly gets the best out of his players.

A quality player himself, mainly throughout the 1980s, he represented top Argentinian clubs like Boca Juniors, River Plate, Vélez Sarsfield and Independiente, and made 20 appearances for Argentina.

His managerial career has taken him to many clubs in the past two decades, mainly in Argentina, Colombia and Brazil before he took charge of Peru in 2015.

His reign has seen the team improve greatly, reaching the semi-finals of the *Copa América* and now qualifying for the 2018 FIFA World Cup.

"I like the group, I think it's an interesting group with very good teams... and all teams who try to play and I think that can fit in well with our characteristics. I think it suits us."

ALL-TIME TOP GOALSCORER
PAOLO GUERRERO
32

ALL-TIME MOST CAPS
ROBERTO PALACIOS
128

HAT-TRICK OF HEROES

ALBERTO RODRÍGUEZ
Any team – particularly an international team – benefits from having a defensive rock to build around. For Peru, that man is Alberto Rodríguez.

The defender has over 70 caps for his national team and, aged 34, he is his nation's most experienced defender.

Much of his club career has been spent in Portugal and back home in Peru with Sporting Club Cristal.

He was part of the Peru squad that came third in the 2011 *Copa América* and has been a mainstay of the side through their recent successes, stepping in as captain on occasion.

JEFFERSON FARFÁN
One of Peru's biggest goal threats is Jefferson Farfán.

The 33-year-old has played for some big clubs around the world and is known for his pace, dribbling and his eye for goal.

Having started his career in his homeland, he really made his name following his move to PSV Eindhoven in the Netherlands. He then had a seven-year spell with Schalke 04 in Germany before stints with Al Jazira, in Abu Dhabi, and Lokomotiv Moscow.

He has won many titles along the way, including four *Eredivisie* championships, the German Cup and the Russian Cup.

PAOLO GUERRERO
Paolo Guerrero is footballing royalty in his homeland and if Peru are to do well at the 2018 FIFA World Cup, they will need him firing on all cylinders.

Guerrero is the country's all-time top goalscorer and has been prolific wherever his career has taken him.

He started off in Germany with Bayern Munich, then had a six-year spell with Hamburger SV before moving to Brazil where he has played for Corinthians and Flamengo.

He has played in four *Copa América* tournaments, finishing top scorer in two, and was the first Peruvian to make the nominees list for the FIFA Ballon d'Or when he did so in 2015.

FIFA World Cup™ Record

Year	Result	Year	Result	Year	Result	Year	Result
1930	R1	1958	DNQ	1978	R2	1998	DNQ
1934	W	1962	DNQ	1982	R1	2002	DNQ
1938	DNE	1966	DNQ	1986	DNQ	2006	DNQ
1950	W	1970	QF	1990	DNQ	2010	DNQ
1954	W	1974	DNQ	1994	DNQ	2014	DNQ

DNE = Did not enter, **DNQ** = Did not qualify, **W** = Withdrew, **R1** = Round 1, **R2** = Round 2, **GS** = Group Stages, **16** = Last 16, **QF** = Quarter-finals, **4th** = Fourth place, **3rd** = Third place, **RU** = Runners-up, **C** = Champions

Statistics up until February 2018

GROUP C
France
Australia
Peru
Denmark

DENMARK

In Denmark's entire FIFA World Cup™ history, they have played 16 matches and scored 27 goals at an average of 1.7 goals per game.

Their fans – and neutrals around the world – are expecting more goals per match than that in Russia this time around and the chances are that those hopes will be answered, and answered emphatically as well.

The 25 goals Denmark scored in their qualification process – including the five they scored in the play-off destruction of Republic of Ireland – should suggest that Russia will see an attacking Danish side this summer.

With brilliant players such as Simon Kjær, Christian Eriksen, Kasper Schmeichel and William Kvist at his disposal, coach Åge Hareide knows Russia is a great opportunity for Denmark to progress further than they ever have before.

The Danes' FIFA World Cup history is not littered with glorious moments and this is only their fifth-ever edition. Their best showing remains their quarter-final effort at the 1998 FIFA World Cup France™, when they narrowly lost 3-2 to eventual finalists Brazil.

The tournaments since then have been hit and miss and they failed to qualify for the 2006 and 2014 editions.

Previous tournaments are all history now and Denmark's young guns are hoping to follow in the footsteps of the likes of Peter Schmeichel and Michael Laudrup and become national icons.

> "It's an incredible feeling and we've been fighting for so long to get there. We've had two very hard play-off games, but with the result we got we can be very pleased. I am looking forward to the World Cup."
> — Christian Eriksen

HOW THEY QUALIFIED

They may have struggled in their qualifying group on the path to the 2018 FIFA World Cup Russia™, but there was nothing to worry about when it came to their crunch play-off encounters with Republic of Ireland last November.

After finishing second in Group E with 20 points, the Danes were held 0-0 by Martin O'Neill's side at home but then went to the Aviva Stadium in the return leg and completely dismantled Ireland 5-1 as a Christian Eriksen hat-trick inspired Denmark to a glorious victory.

It is fair to say that not even Denmark's biggest supporters saw a performance of that magnitude on the horizon but the Danes proved they can perform at their best when the pressure is on.

In the earlier qualifying stages, Denmark conceded only eight goals in ten matches, by far the best record in the group, to underline their defensive prowess as they finished five points behind Poland.

France
Australia
Peru
Denmark

GROUP C

ALL-TIME TOP GOALSCORER
POUL NIELSEN/ JON DAHL TOMASSON
52

ALL-TIME MOST CAPS
PETER SCHMEICHEL
152

THE COACH

ÅGE HAREIDE

When Morten Olsen stepped down as Denmark's longest-serving manager after they failed to qualify for UEFA EURO 2016, the Danes turned to a man who knows Scandinavian football inside out.

Åge Hareide played 50 times for Norway as a central defender in the 1970s and 80s; he also managed his national team for five years between 2003 and 2008 and he has achieved domestic success at the likes of Molde, Rosenborg and Malmö.

Hareide's philosophy is based on constant attack and pressure. He wants his team to play with freedom and a goalscoring mindset and his attempts to transform Denmark into a team that looks to go on the offensive appear to be working well.

> "I have always been very offensively minded as a coach. I want to attack the play. The main purpose of football is to score goals; that is the same intention that I have at club or national team."

HAT-TRICK OF HEROES

CHRISTIAN ERIKSEN

Christian Eriksen has been hailed by both his Tottenham Hotspur manager Mauricio Pochettino and national boss Åge Hareide as one of the world's greatest talents at the moment – and with good reason.

The midfielder continues to get better and better, and his hat-trick against the Republic of Ireland proves he loves scoring goals as much as he enjoys making them, and he is the true heartbeat of the Danish side.

If Denmark are to perform at their best at the 2018 FIFA World Cup Russia, then there is absolutely no doubt that Eriksen will need to be performing at his usual impeccable best.

KASPER SCHMEICHEL

Kasper Schmeichel may have spent the early part of his career trying to escape from the shadow of his legendary father, Peter, but that is no longer the case.

Schmeichel was in stunning form during Leicester City's fairy-tale Premier League-winning season in 2015-16 and he has become a fine goalkeeper in his own right.

Although he is not the tallest of goalkeepers, he commands his box and he is a superb shot-stopper and organiser.

All good defences need a solid goalkeeper behind them and Denmark are luckier than most.

SIMON KJÆR

Simon Kjær is a superbly efficient central defender for Sevilla in *La Liga* and his defensive prowess has been rewarded with the captaincy of his country.

He is a key performer for the Spanish side and Denmark also look to him to provide solidity and consistency at the back.

He is at the peak of his career at present and will do whatever it takes to try and ensure Denmark have a strong defensive base to launch attacks from.

Kjær is cool, calm and collected on the ball and offers confidence to those around him.

FIFA World Cup™ Record

1930	DNE	1958	DNQ	1978	DNQ	1998	QF
1934	DNE	1962	DNE	1982	DNQ	2002	16
1938	DNE	1966	DNQ	1986	16	2006	DNQ
1950	DNE	1970	DNQ	1990	DNQ	2010	GS
1954	DNE	1974	DNQ	1994	DNQ	2014	DNQ

DNE = Did not enter, **DNQ** = Did not qualify, **W** = Withdrew, **R1** = Round 1, **R2** = Round 2, **GS** = Group Stages, **16** = Last 16, **QF** = Quarter-finals, **4th** = Fourth place, **3rd** = Third place, **RU** = Runners-up, **C** = Champions

Statistics up until February 2018

ARGENTINA

ICELAND

CROATIA

NIGERIA

FIFA WORLD CUP RUSSIA 2018

Group D Fixtures

16 JUNE
Argentina v. Iceland
14:00
Spartak Stadium, Moscow

16 JUNE
Croatia v. Nigeria
20:00
Kaliningrad Stadium, Kaliningrad

21 JUNE
Argentina v. Croatia
19:00
Nizhny Novgorod Stadium, Nizhny Novgorod

22 JUNE
Nigeria v. Iceland
16:00
Volgograd Arena, Volgograd

26 JUNE
Iceland v. Croatia
19:00
Rostov Arena, Rostov-on-Don

26 JUNE
Nigeria v. Argentina
19:00
Saint Petersburg Stadium, Saint Petersburg

Kick-offs are UK time (UTC/GMT)

GROUP D
- Argentina
- Iceland
- Croatia
- Nigeria

ARGENTINA

Argentina will go into the 2018 FIFA World Cup Russia™ as they always do – as one of the favourites to win the tournament.

Their history in the competition and the talent they have in the squad means they will be tipped by football enthusiasts around the globe to go all the way and lift the official trophy on 15 July.

With names like Mascherano, Agüero, Banega, Di María, Dybala and, of course, Messi in their ranks, the *Albiceleste* will be confident they can compete with the best on the planet, but they will have the weight of history on their shoulders as they look to emulate Argentinian legends of the past.

Twice before Argentina have ruled the world, first as hosts in 1978, then eight years later in Mexico, and they have been runners-up three times – in 1930, 1990 and 2014.

The 1978 victory really put Argentina on the football map and created memories that will last forever as a Mario Kempes double helped them to a 3-1 extra-time victory on a ticker tape-covered pitch.

Then began the Diego Maradona era. As he reached the peak of his powers in 1986, he inspired his team to knockout victories over Uruguay, England and Belgium before edging past the mighty West Germany 3-2 at the Estadio Azteca in Mexico City.

Four years later, West Germany got their revenge by squeezing out Argentina 1-0 in the final in Rome.

Now the boot is on the other foot. Four years after losing the 2014 final to Germany, could Argentina exact the sweetest revenge of all in Moscow?

> *"It would have been crazy not to be in the World Cup. The group deserved to qualify."*
> — ✦ Lionel Messi ✦

HOW THEY QUALIFIED

Considering the wealth of talent at their disposal, Argentina certainly made their fans sweat during a rollercoaster qualification campaign.

Needing to finish in the top four of a ten-team South American group, the Argentinians went into the final round of matches in sixth place, needing to win their final game and hope results elsewhere went their way.

Things would have been a lot simpler had they won either of their two previous home games against Venezuela and Peru, which both ended up as draws.

It went down to an away game at Ecuador and a Messi-inspired Argentina played their part, as his hat-trick ensured his team claimed a a 3-1 victory.

Luckily for the *Albiceleste*, results elsewhere couldn't have gone much better for them and they effectively swapped positions with third-placed Chile, who lost 3-0 against Brazil.

A potential disaster had been averted. Time to look forward.

Argentina
Iceland
Croatia
Nigeria

GROUP D

FIFA WORLD CUP RUSSIA 2018

ALL-TIME TOP GOALSCORER
LIONEL MESSI
61

ALL-TIME MOST CAPS
JAVIER ZANETTI
143

THE COACH

JORGE SAMPAOLI

As a coach, if you want to endear yourself to your new fans after taking over the Argentina national team, first results don't get much better than beating Brazil.

It may only have been a friendly, but every game between these two footballing powerhouses counts – and Sampaoli got off to the best possible start with a 1-0 win.

The Argentine's coaching career began in club football in Peru, followed by spells in Chile and Ecuador.

He then landed the Chile job, leading the country to its first ever *Copa América* title in 2015, which impressed Sevilla enough to offer him a contract.

A short but successful stint in Spain was cut short when Argentina came calling in May 2017.

> "The only thing I can tell our fans is that we will make Argentina proud. I also have the best player in history; that's always a plus."

HAT-TRICK OF HEROES

SERGIO ROMERO

He may not always have been first-choice goalkeeper for his clubs over the years but there's no doubting Sergio Romero's pedigree at international level.

The Manchester United man is closing in on 100 caps for his country, having made his debut for Argentina back in 2009. Since then, every national team coach has fully backed him.

Romero has played his club football for Racing Club, AZ Alkmaar, Sampdoria, and Monaco, and joined United in 2015.

He made himself a national hero when his penalty saves helped Argentina beat the Netherlands in the 2014 FIFA World Cup™ semi-finals.

JAVIER MASCHERANO

If you've been a regular in the Argentina national team for around 15 years, you must have something special about you.

Javier Mascherano is nicknamed *El Jefecito*, meaning "The Little Chief", and he plays with the authority and commitment of someone who was born to lead.

His early club career was played in South America with River Plate and Corinthians before a move to England to play for West Ham and then Liverpool.

He then signed for Barcelona, where he was switched from a midfielder to a defender, and went on to win multiple *La Liga* and Champions League titles.

LIONEL MESSI

If ever a man carried the hopes of a nation on his shoulders, it is Lionel Messi and Argentina.

The *Albiceleste* skipper is considered by some to be the best player ever to grace a football pitch and his goal record is phenomenal. He holds the records for the most goals in *La Liga*, in a *La Liga* season, a club football season in Europe and a calendar year.

It's not all about his goals though as he holds the record for the most assists in *La Liga* history.

A multiple FIFA Ballon d'Or winner, he has won almost everything there is to win – including an Olympic gold medal in 2008. There's only one obvious trophy missing…

FIFA World Cup™ Record

1930	RU	1958	GS	1978	C	1998	QF
1934	R1	1962	GS	1982	R2	2002	GS
1938	W	1966	QF	1986	C	2006	QF
1950	W	1970	DNQ	1990	RU	2010	QF
1954	W	1974	R2	1994	16	2014	RU

DNE = Did not enter, **DNQ** = Did not qualify, **W** = Withdrew, **R1** = Round 1, **R2** = Round 2, **GS** = Group Stages, **16** = Last 16, **QF** = Quarter-finals, **4th** = Fourth place, **3rd** = Third place, **RU** = Runners-up, **C** = Champions

Statistics up until February 2018

OFFICIAL 2018 FIFA WORLD CUP™ TOURNAMENT MAGAZINE **81**

GROUP D
Argentina
Iceland
Croatia
Nigeria

ICELAND

For every nation taking part in the 2018 FIFA World Cup™ it will be a historic occasion, but for some countries it will mean that little bit more.

Iceland are taking part in their first-ever FIFA World Cup™ in Russia and their excitement couldn't be any greater because, for Icelandic football fans, this is the best time to be alive.

Having not qualified for any major tournaments in their history, Iceland came within a whisker of making it to the 2014 FIFA World Cup Brazil™, coming second in their group and advancing to a play-off with Croatia, which they lost 2-0 on aggregate.

Not to be deterred, they went one better in their next qualifying campaign, this time for UEFA EURO 2016, finishing second in their group and beating the Netherlands twice along the way.

That was only the start of their adventure. In the finals themselves, Iceland qualified from their group, drawing with Portugal and Hungary before beating Austria to set up a round-of-16 clash with England.

There followed another piece of Icelandic history as the team secured a remarkable 2-1 victory before succumbing to France in the quarter-finals.

Now they have qualified for the FIFA World Cup for the first time in their history, becoming the smallest nation ever to make it, with a population of only around 330,000.

They are a team that have their whole country united behind them and writing them off would be a big mistake.

> "This is an incredibly difficult group. Argentina have one of the strongest squads in football... and the Nigerian players are great athletes."
> — ✦ Aron Gunnarsson ✦

HOW THEY QUALIFIED

Iceland bounced into their 2018 FIFA World Cup qualifying campaign full of confidence after their eye-catching performances at UEFA EURO 2016 and that momentum carried them to the top of the appropriately-named Group I.

In a group that contained tricky opponents like Croatia, Ukraine, Turkey and Finland, plus Kosovo, they finished two points clear of the Croats, who had to qualify via the play-offs instead.

Iceland only lost two of their ten qualifiers – away at Finland and Croatia – but won all five of their home matches to dominate the group.

In the end, they just needed to win their final match, at home to Kosovo, which they did 2-0 with goals from Gylfi Sigurdsson and Johann Gudmundsson, to secure their place in the history books.

Everton midfielder Sigurdsson top-scored for Iceland in qualifying matches with four goals to cement his status as a national hero.

Argentina
Iceland
Croatia
Nigeria

GROUP D

FIFA WORLD CUP RUSSIA 2018

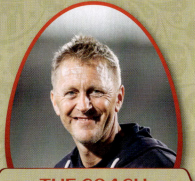

THE COACH

HEIMIR HALLGRÍMSSON

The route Heimir Hallgrímsson has taken to coaching his national team at the 2018 FIFA World Cup is different to every other coach in the tournament.

After a career as a player in Iceland, he first began coaching the Höttur women's team while he was still playing for the men's team.

While still continuing a part-time career as a dentist, he later had spells as manager of both the ÍBV men's and women's teams before being appointed assistant manager to Lars Lagerbäck with the Iceland national team in 2011.

In 2013 he became joint manager with Lagerbäck and when the Swede left in 2016, Hallgrímsson was placed in sole charge.

> "When you think about the World Cup, you think about Argentina and Brazil, so it's a little bit of a romantic feeling to play Argentina in the first game."

ALL-TIME TOP GOALSCORER
EIDUR GUDJOHNSEN
26

ALL-TIME MOST CAPS
RÚNAR KRISTINSSON
104

HAT-TRICK OF HEROES

RAGNAR SIGURDSSON

Centre-back Ragnar Sigurdsson is one of the rocks Iceland's recent success has been built on.

After starting his career at Fylkir, he spent four years with IFK Göteborg, winning several major honours, and was watched by several clubs from Europe's biggest leagues.

He added to his medal collection at FC Copenhagen before moving to Krasnodar in Russia. From there he moved to Fulham, but spent much of last season at Rubin Kazan.

A solid defender with good ability in the air, his greatest moment for his national team probably came when he scored against England in that famous 2-1 win during UEFA EURO 2016.

ARON GUNNARSSON

The Iceland captain is one of the mainstays in Heimir Hallgrímsson's squad and his elevation to skipper has coincided with the strongest period in Iceland's footballing history.

Gunnarsson was handed the armband in 2012 and since then Iceland have qualified for both the European Championships and the FIFA World Cup.

Normally operating as a midfielder, Gunnarsson has played for AZ Alkmaar and Coventry City, and has been at Cardiff City since 2011. There, he played in the 2012 League Cup final, gained promotion to the Premier League and has been one of their most important players.

GYLFI SIGURDSSON

The golden boy of Icelandic football is rated so highly that Everton paid around £40 million for his services last summer.

The attacking midfielder is a set-piece specialist whose crosses create havoc in opposing penalty areas and he has the ability to score directly from free-kicks too.

Sigurdsson has travelled extensively and been popular at many of his clubs, being named player of the year at Reading, Hoffenheim and Swansea City.

For the national team, he has clocked up more than 50 caps and among his highlights, he scored all the goals as Iceland won both 2-0 and 1-0 against the Netherlands in qualifying matches for UEFA EURO 2016.

FIFA World Cup™ Record

1930	DNE	1958	DNQ	1978	DNQ	1998	DNQ
1934	DNE	1962	DNE	1982	DNQ	2002	DNQ
1938	DNE	1966	DNE	1986	DNQ	2006	DNQ
1950	DNE	1970	DNE	1990	DNQ	2010	DNQ
1954	DNE	1974	DNQ	1994	DNQ	2014	DNQ

DNE = Did not enter, **DNQ** = Did not qualify, **W** = Withdrew, **R1** = Round 1, **R2** = Round 2, **GS** = Group Stages, **16** = Last 16, **QF** = Quarter-finals, **4th** = Fourth place, **3rd** = Third place, **RU** = Runners-up, **C** = Champions

Statistics up until February 2018

GROUP D
Argentina
Iceland
Croatia
Nigeria

CROATIA

Croatia were only admitted into FIFA in 1993, having previously been a part of Yugoslavia. That meant they could not play at the 1994 FIFA World Cup USA™ because they were too late to qualify.

However, they have more than made up for lost time.

In the pantheon of Croatian greats, names likes Davor Šuker and Zvonimir Boban are key names, especially as they helped take Croatia to third at the 1998 FIFA World Cup France™. They are footballing legends at home but there is no reason why the new breed of Croatian performers cannot excel themselves – and perhaps become even greater national heroes.

That 1998 edition was Croatia's best finish so far at a FIFA World Cup™ and although they failed to qualify in 2010, they have been a fixture at every other tournament since.

With the coaching stint of Ante Čačić now a distant memory, belief in the Croatia squad has grown and the endless formation tinkering that underlined Čačić's managerial reign is likely to be replaced by a more consistent style of play under Zlatko Dalić.

One look at the Croatia squad helps prove just how much potential it has and it appears to be crammed with aggressive ball-winners, talented midfielders, strong defenders and some fine goalkeepers.

Bringing all those factors together will be crucial if Croatia are to eclipse the class of 1998 but one thing is for sure; every side they face will have to be at their best if they want to overcome Croatia's talented, streetwise and determined side.

> "We have all done a good job. Croatia is a great country and most importantly we are at the World Cup."
> — ✦ Luka Modrić ✦

HOW THEY QUALIFIED

Having finished in second spot in Group I behind Iceland, Croatia had to run the gauntlet of the play-offs to seal their place at the 2018 FIFA World Cup Russia™.

The qualifiers were an inconsistent affair for Croatia as they won six of their ten matches, drawing two and losing the remaining two. They had the best goal difference in Group I (+11) but Iceland won a game more, meaning Croatia had to beat Greece to get to Russia.

Yet any doubts about Croatia's ability to control the nerves associated with play-off football did not last long at all.

Over the two legs, Croatia were more than a match for Greece and a wonderful 4-1 victory in the first leg in Zagreb in November last year virtually guaranteed their qualification.

A goalless draw in Greece confirmed it, and Croatia were on their way, much to the delight of the entire football-mad country.

Now they have a second chance to try and finish above Iceland, having been grouped with them once again.

Argentina
Iceland
Croatia
Nigeria

GROUP **D**

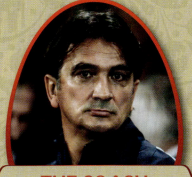

THE COACH

ALL-TIME TOP GOALSCORER
DAVOR ŠUKER
45

ALL-TIME MOST CAPS
DARIJO SRNA
134

HAT-TRICK OF HEROES

LUKA MODRIĆ

Luka Modrić is the heartbeat of Croatia's squad and starting XI. He currently plays for Real Madrid after moving there from Tottenham Hotspur in 2012.

Although diminutive in stature, Modrić's talents on the ball more than make up for his lack of physicality.

He has become a firm favourite in *La Liga* for his willingness to get forward when he can and doing his best to unlock opposition defences.

Real Madrid have world-class performers all over the pitch but few are as consistent and as enjoyable to watch as Modrić, who appears to be getting better with every passing season.

ZLATKO DALIĆ

He has not been in charge long but Zlatko Dalić's reign as Croatia manager has seen its fair share of celebration and glory.

He was only brought in in October 2017 as a replacement for Ante Čačić, who left with Croatia's passage to the 2018 FIFA World Cup Russia™ looking exceptionally precarious indeed.

However, the former midfielder oversaw Croatia's success and is feted in his homeland as a result.

Dalić has had a long managerial career and he recently spent time in Saudi Arabia and the United Arab Emirates before answering Croatia's call in the most emphatic of manners.

> "I did not have to do much. I mostly talked to my players. This qualification is also as much down to the previous coach and comes as a result of his work. We are a very good team and failure to qualify for the World Cup was not an option."

DEJAN LOVREN

Dejan Lovren is an integral performer for Liverpool in the Premier League and his tall, physical style of play means he is well suited to the English game.

Lovren is a central defender with good pace and he is a clever reader of the game.

Croatia will need some tough leaders if they are to thrive in Russia and Lovren could be key to those aims.

Lovren enjoys the tussle involved with playing in defence and is also an impressive header of the ball.

Croatia look to him for solidity at the back and he is rarely found wanting.

NIKOLA KALINIĆ

When Nikola Kalinić was ruled out of Croatia's qualifiers against Finland and Ukraine last October, Croatia's fans were devastated at the prospect of coping without him and that underlines his worth to his national side.

Kalinić, who plays his domestic football in *Serie A*, will have to shoulder a lot of Croatia's goalscoring responsibility at the 2018 FIFA World Cup Russia but he has never shied away from a challenge in the past and it is unlikely that he will start now.

Kalinić simply loves scoring goals and getting forward, and no defender in Russia will fancy their chances of keeping him quiet if he is on song.

FIFA World Cup™ Record

1930	DNE	1958	DNE	1978	DNE	1998	3rd
1934	DNE	1962	DNE	1982	DNE	2002	GS
1938	DNE	1966	DNE	1986	DNE	2006	GS
1950	DNE	1970	DNE	1990	DNE	2010	DNQ
1954	DNE	1974	DNE	1994	DNE	2014	GS

DNE = Did not enter, **DNQ** = Did not qualify, **W** = Withdrew, **R1** = Round 1, **R2** = Round 2, **GS** = Group Stages, **16** = Last 16, **QF** = Quarter-finals, **4th** = Fourth place, **3rd** = Third place, **RU** = Runners-up, **C** = Champions

Statistics up until February 2018

GROUP D
- Argentina
- Iceland
- Croatia
- **Nigeria**

NIGERIA

Nigeria are among the most consistent footballing nations in the world and are getting used to flying the flag for Africa at the FIFA World Cup™.

The *Super Eagles* have qualified for six out of the last seven FIFA World Cups and first captured the world's attention when they appeared at the 1994 FIFA World Cup™ in the USA.

On their first outing at the world's greatest tournament they topped a group containing Argentina, Greece and Bulgaria, and they were two minutes away from knocking Italy out at the round-of-16 stage, but eventually lost out in extra time.

In their four subsequent appearances they haven't managed to better that performance, though they also reached the last 16 in 1998 and four years ago in Brazil.

That most recent appearance saw them beat Bosnia and draw against IR Iran to qualify from the group, but they lost an exciting last-16 encounter to Argentina.

Their performances in the Africa Cup of Nations also mark them out as one of the continent's most powerful footballing nations. They are Africa's fourth most successful country in the competition, having won it in 1980, 1994 and 2013.

Claiming the title in 1994 helped Nigeria into fifth place in the FIFA world rankings, the highest position an African nation has ever held.

Now a new and exciting era is emerging under German coach Gernot Rohr. A fresh, young squad is ready to show what it can do, with captain John Obi Mikel leading the way.

> "Hunger for success drove us to beat Zambia and qualify. I am proud of the players and we are ready for the World Cup."
> — ✦ John Obi Mikel ✦

HOW THEY QUALIFIED

Nigeria were the first African nation to qualify for the 2018 FIFA World Cup™ when they beat Zambia 1-0 in their fifth Group B match, thanks to a goal from Arsenal's Alex Iwobi in Uyo.

The group the *Super Eagles* were drawn in was considered to be very tough so the fact they qualified so comfortably, going unbeaten and finishing six points clear of Zambia (although they were later docked several points for fielding an ineligible player) was very impressive.

The highlight of the qualifiers had to be a 4-0 win over Cameroon – the only defeat the *Indomitable Lions* suffered during the campaign.

Their goals were scored largely by players familiar to Premier League viewers. Victor Moses scored three times in the group while Alex Iwobi, Kelechi Iheanacho and former Chelsea midfielder John Obi Mikel got two goals each.

Nigeria will hope the goals continue to flow in Russia.

Argentina
Iceland
Croatia
Nigeria

GROUP D

ALL-TIME TOP GOALSCORER
RASHIDI YEKINI
37

ALL-TIME MOST CAPS
VINCENT ENYEAMA, JOSEPH YOBO
101

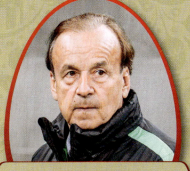

THE COACH

GERNOT ROHR

The name Gernot Rohr might not be too familiar around the globe but the Nigeria coach has a long and fairly impressive CV.

After a playing career that included a spell with Bayern Munich and a 12-year stretch at Bordeaux, he went on to coach the French club – and that was just the beginning.

The best part of three decades in football management has seen him at clubs like Nice, Young Boys, Ajaccio and Nantes, but in recent years he has concentrated on African football, leading Gabon, Niger and Burkina Faso.

He knows what he's doing and the qualifying campaign for the 2018 FIFA World Cup could not have gone much better.

"It's a new challenge, a new adventure that's coming. Participating in the most important tournament in the world, with the best teams, is something every player and coach dreams about."

HAT-TRICK OF HEROES

JOHN OBI MIKEL

The old head of the Nigeria squad seems to have been around forever but John Obi Mikel is still in the prime of his career and has plenty of attributes to offer his team at the 2018 FIFA World Cup.

He is best known for his time at Chelsea where he spent over a decade and won two Premier League titles, four FA Cups, the UEFA Champions League and the UEFA Europa League, plus lots more.

Not known as a goalscorer, he did manage a couple of goals in qualifying, but he is best recognised as a reliable ball-winner with a calm presence in midfield.

ALEX IWOBI

When the 2018 FIFA World Cup kicks off, Alex Iwobi will only just have turned 22, yet he already plays with the maturity and ability of a more experienced player.

The nephew of Nigerian hero Jay-Jay Okocha, footballing ability clearly runs in the family and his impressive development has been overseen by veteran Arsenal manager Arsene Wenger since Iwobi's first appearance for the *Gunners* back in October 2015.

Goals are his game and he already has several for Nigeria, including the goal against Zambia that sealed the country's 2018 FIFA World Cup place.

AHMED MUSA

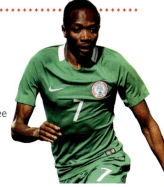

The Leicester City forward, who has been on loan at CSKA Moscow, has lightning in his boots and enough pace to scare any defender.

Aged just 25 and with more than 60 caps already in the bag, it seems well within the bounds of reality that he could end up beating the national record of 101 appearances.

His goal record is pretty impressive too. He scored a goal every three games during four years at CSKA Moscow, but the Premier League is still waiting to see the best of him after his move to the Foxes.

He holds the distinction of being the first Nigerian to score more than once in a FIFA World Cup match after netting twice against Argentina in 2014.

FIFA World Cup™ Record

1930	DNE	1958	DNE	1978	DNQ	1998	16
1934	DNE	1962	DNQ	1982	DNQ	2002	GS
1938	DNE	1966	W	1986	DNQ	2006	DNQ
1950	DNE	1970	DNQ	1990	DNQ	2010	GS
1954	DNE	1974	DNQ	1994	16	2014	16

DNE = Did not enter, **DNQ** = Did not qualify, **W** = Withdrew, **R1** = Round 1, **R2** = Round 2, **GS** = Group Stages, **16** = Last 16, **QF** = Quarter-finals, **4ᵗʰ** = Fourth place, **3ʳᵈ** = Third place, **RU** = Runners-up, **C** = Champions

Statistics up until February 2018

2014 adidas FIFA World Cup™ Golden Boot winner James Rodríguez with his prize

WILL THE ADIDAS GOLDEN BOOT BE ON ANOTHER FOOT?

Goal kings set to battle for a place in FIFA World Cup™ history

Just Fontaine, Eusébio, Gerd Müller, Paolo Rossi, Ronaldo… the names are forever etched in football history.

They were all goalscorers of fine repute – some even had legendary status – but the moment they won the adidas Golden Boot for being top goalscorer at a World Cup, the legacy of their careers reached a new level.

At the 2018 FIFA World Cup™ in Russia, the race for the adidas Golden Boot starts all over again and some of the world's finest goalscorers will be in contention.

Every country has a main goal threat and the wealth of talent on display in Russia will be such that the trophy could be carried off by any one of dozens of contenders.

Being in a team that is likely to progress to the latter stages of the tournament will help, but in some cases a flurry of early goals can be crucial.

Take the case of Russia's Oleg Salenko at the 1994 FIFA World Cup USA™. He ended up as joint-top goalscorer with Bulgaria's Hristo Stoichkov, despite his team being knocked out in the group stage. Six goals in his three appearances were enough to make the difference, with five of them coming in an amazing 6-1 win over Cameroon.

In fact, it's strange to note that in the 20 editions of the FIFA World Cup™ so far, on only five occasions has a winner or joint winner of the adidas Golden Boot also been part of the team that has won the tournament.

The king of the Golden Boot winners would have to be France's Just Fontaine, who scored an incredible 13 goals at the 1958 FIFA World Cup™, which included a hat-trick against Paraguay in the group stages and a four-goal haul in the third-place play-off against West Germany.

The first FIFA World Cup™ top scorer was Guillermo Stábile in 1930, who hit eight goals, while other big names to have achieved the honour include Gary Lineker, Mario Kempes, Miroslav Klose, Sándor Kocsis and Salvatore Totò Schillaci.

The current holder of the award is Colombia's James Rodríguez. He scored six goals in Brazil four years ago, including the goal of the tournament, when his outstanding volley crashed in off the crossbar against Uruguay.

Fitness permitting, he'll be back to try and win the trophy again in Russia. If he does, he'll feel the same pride he felt in 2014 when he received an award that he had a special place reserved for. He said at the time: "It's going home and that's where it's going to stay. It's for life."

And when asked about that glorious strike against Uruguay, he added: "I've seen it … (pauses and smiles) about 20 times. I always try it in training. You try 100 times and it goes in twice."

ADIDAS GOLDEN BOOT

Thomas Müller in 2010

adidas FIFA World Cup™ Golden Boot winners

- **2014:** James Rodríguez (Colombia) 6 goals
- **2010:** Thomas Müller (Germany) 5 goals
- **2006:** Miroslav Klose (Germany) 5 goals
- **2002:** Ronaldo (Brazil) 8 goals
- **1998:** Davor Šuker (Croatia) 6 goals
- **1994:** Hristo Stoichkov (Bulgaria), Oleg Salenko (Russia) 6 goals
- **1990:** Salvatore Schillaci (Italy) 6 goals
- **1986:** Gary Lineker (England) 6 goals
- **1982:** Paolo Rossi (Italy) 6 goals
- **1978:** Mario Kempes (Argentina) 6 goals
- **1974:** Grzegorz Lato (Poland) 7 goals
- **1970:** Gerd Müller (Germany) 10 goals
- **1966:** Eusébio (Portugal) 9 goals
- **1962:** Flórián Albert (Hungary), Valentin Ivanov (Soviet Union), Dražan Jerković (Yugoslavia), Leonel Sánchez (Chile), Vavá (Brazil), Garrincha (Brazil) All 4 goals
- **1958:** Just Fontaine (France) 13 goals
- **1954:** Sándor Kocsis (Hungary) 11 goals
- **1950:** Ademir (Brazil) 8 goals
- **1938:** Leônidas (Brazil) 8 goals
- **1934:** Oldřich Nejedlý (Czechoslovakia) 5 goals
- **1930:** Guillermo Stábile (Argentina) 8 goals

Mario Kempes in 1978

Ronaldo in 2002

JAMES RODRÍGUEZ BRAZIL 2014 ADIDAS GOLDEN BOOT WINNER

6 GOALS

ADIDAS GOLDEN BOOT

Rodríguez struck the goal of the tournament in 2014

Rodríguez doesn't see that goal as being any more important than any of the others he scored in Brazil, though.

"I like all six. They were all important because they helped the team to win games. Every one of them was special because scoring goals in such a big competition is unique. The Golden Boot is a dream come true."

If Rodríguez is to win the award again, he'll have beaten some top-quality players to do so.

Thomas Müller of Germany will surely have a big say in the destination of the trophy. He won the adidas Golden Boot at the 2010 FIFA World Cup™ in South Africa and was only one goal behind Rodríguez in Brazil.

Germany will be going to Russia expecting to progress a long way in the tournament and with a total of 10 World Cup finals goals already to his name, Müller might even be eyeing the all-time record of 16, currently held by compatriot Klose.

The two players generally considered to be the best in the world, Lionel Messi and Cristiano Ronaldo, will both believe that one thing missing from their hugely impressive CVs is a FIFA World Cup™ adidas Golden Boot award. Both are in teams with a chance of doing well at the tournament.

Ronaldo managed 15 goals during Portugal's qualifying campaign and both he and Messi know a profitable FIFA World Cup campaign will put them in pole position when the big personal awards are handed out at the end of the year.

The only player who outscored Ronaldo in the European qualifying campaign was Poland's Robert Lewandowski. He hit 16 goals and has been one of the world's sharpest shooters for many years.

Elsewhere in Europe, the big threats to Rodríguez's crown could come from France's Antoine Griezmann, Belgium's Romelu Lukaku, England's Harry Kane or Spain's Álvaro Morata, while Denmark's Christian Eriksen continues to prove that you don't have to be recognised as a striker to consistently get among the goals.

Brazil will be many people's favourites to win the tournament and with a strike force that includes the brilliant Neymar, Gabriel Jesus and Philippe Coutinho, it's easy to see why. Any one of those could finish as the tournament's top scorer while South America will also be represented by talented goal-getters like Sergio Agüero, Edinson Cavani and Luis Suárez.

Saudi Arabia's Mohammed Al-Sahlawi hit 16 goals in qualifying and will be one of Asia's main hopes of hitting the goal trail in Russia, while Africa has a wealth of striking talent including Senegal's Sadio Mané, Egypt's Mohamed Salah and Nigeria's Ahmed Musa.

An honourable mention too for Australia's Tim Cahill, who, at 38, carries the hopes of his nation, having hit a half-century of goals for his country, five of them in three different World Cups between 2006-14.

Then there's the host nation, who will be hoping Fyodor Smolov's goals can take them into the knockout rounds.

Of course, there's a chance that the adidas Golden Boot will go to a player who hasn't been mentioned in this article, and that is the beauty of the unpredictability of football.

Whoever does win it will join a pantheon of greats that will be remembered for generations to come.

Could Fyodor Smolov be an adidas Golden Boot contender this time around?

When the world comes together, the game comes alive.

Qatar Airways is proud to be the official airline partner of FIFA, bringing fans from over 150 destinations to the 2018 FIFA World Cup Russia.™

ALL TOGETHER NOW

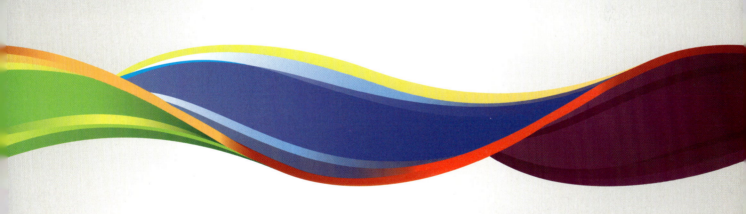

FIFA WORLD CUP
RUSSIA 2018

QATAR AIRWAYS

OFFICIAL AIRLINE PARTNER

qatarairways.com

Luzhniki Stadium

Host City:
Moscow

Project:
Stadium reconstruction

Location:
Luzhniki Sports Complex

Home team:
Russia

DEVELOPMENT
The main stadium for Russia 2018 was originally built to host the first nationwide summer Spartakiad in 1956. Since then, Luzhniki Stadium has hosted a multitude of major sporting and cultural events, including the 1980 Summer Olympics, world championships in ice hockey, athletics and rugby, and concerts.

DESIGN
Work to rebuild Luzhniki Stadium for Russia 2018 began in 2013. One of the crucial aspects of the project was to preserve the historic look of the stadium, which has become one of Moscow's true landmarks. Inside, the stadium has been totally refurbished: the athletics track has been removed, the stands moved closer to the pitch, their gradient adjusted and two extra tiers added.

CITY
Founded in the 12th century, Moscow is the capital of the Russian Federation and one of the most renowned and fascinating cities in the world. It is a dynamic 21st century metropolis. Luzhniki Stadium is located at the centre of Moscow's 145-hectare Olympic complex, one of the largest sports complexes in the world.

Samara Arena

Host City:
Samara

Project:
New stadium

Location:
Radiotsentr district

Home team:
FC Krylya Sovetov

DEVELOPMENT
The new Samara Arena has been built in the Radiotsentr district, surrounded by a residential development and high-quality infrastructure. In 2014, Russian President Vladimir Putin took part in a time-capsule ceremony marking the start of construction. After Russia 2018, the stadium will be home to FC Krylya Sovetov.

DESIGN
Samara Arena's design concept is dominated by the theme of space as a tribute to the traditions of the region and its renowned aerospace sector. The shape of the stadium resembles a glass dome. In the evening, the whole structure will be lit up, emphasising the stadium's expressive design.

CITY
Samara is the capital of the Samara Region and home to 1.1 million people. It is one of the most prominent Volga region cities and is known as Russia's aerospace centre. During World War II, Samara became the "second capital" of Russia as all government departments were evacuated here from Moscow. One of Samara's iconic landmarks is a 68-metre monument of the Soyuz carrier rocket, built to commemorate Yuri Gagarin's space flight.

Rostov Arena

Host City:
Rostov-on-Don

Project:
New stadium

Location:
Left bank of the Don River, the Grebnoy canal area

Home team:
FC Rostov

DEVELOPMENT
Rostov Arena is situated on the left bank of the Don River. Buoyed by its selection as a host city, Rostov-on-Don has been able to expand in size by developing its left bank, where the local tourism facilities and restaurants are now a major attraction. After Russia 2018, FC Rostov, the 2014 Russian Cup winners, will play its home games here.

DESIGN
Rostov Arena's original design blends harmoniously into the picturesque landscape. The shape of the arena's roof imitates the meanderings of the Don River. The varying heights of the stands allow spectators to savour not only what is happening on the pitch, but also to enjoy views of Rostov-on-Don.

CITY
Known from the time of Herodotus as a land of warlike Scythians, the endless steppes of the Don river basin eventually became home to the freedom-loving Cossacks. The flamboyant Cossack culture is still prevalent in Rostov-on-Don, a modern city of one million inhabitants overlooking the beautiful Don River. The city is a key transport and cultural hub of southern Russia.

Saint Petersburg Stadium

Host City:
Saint Petersburg

Project:
New stadium

Location:
Krestovsky Island

Home team:
FC Zenit Saint Petersburg

DEVELOPMENT

Saint Petersburg's new, super-modern stadium has been built on the site of the old Kirov Stadium on Krestovsky Island, which, in its day, was one of the country's largest stadiums with a capacity of 110,000. The tender to build Saint Petersburg Stadium was won by famous Japanese architect Kisho Kurokawa. The stadium will be home to Zenit Saint Petersburg.

DESIGN

The architect's vision for Saint Petersburg Stadium is of a spaceship that has landed on the shores of the Gulf of Finland. Technologically, Saint Petersburg Stadium is one of the world's most modern arenas. Equipped with a retractable roof and a sliding pitch, it is able to host any type of event.

CITY

Founded by Peter the Great in 1703 as Russia's new imperial capital, Saint Petersburg is the ultimate embodiment of artistic talent with the best architects and artists from Russia and Europe leaving their mark. Saint Petersburg city centre is a UNESCO World Heritage site. Saint Petersburg welcomes up to five million tourists each year, more than any other city in Russia.

Spartak Stadium

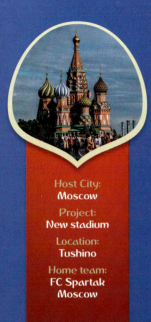

Host City:
Moscow
Project:
New stadium
Location:
Tushino
Home team:
FC Spartak Moscow

DEVELOPMENT
Spartak Moscow, the "people's team", are one of Russia's most popular football clubs and yet, despite being founded in 1922, they have always had to make do without their own stadium. In spring 2010, however, Spartak started building their own stadium on the site of Moscow's former airfield in the district of Tushino. The venue hosted its first match in 2014 when Spartak played Red Star Belgrade.

DESIGN
Spartak Stadium's appearance is a matter of great pride. Its design takes the form of chain mail consisting of hundreds of little diamonds representing the Spartak logo. The colours of these diamonds can be changed depending on which team is playing.

CITY
Moscow welcomes over four million tourists each year. Home to over 130 nationalities and 12.3 million residents, Moscow is served by three international airports and the world's second busiest underground system. Moscow is blessed with beautiful architecture and such renowned cultural landmarks as the Bolshoi Theatre, the Kremlin and the Pushkin Fine Arts Museum, to name but a few.

Mordovia Arena

Host City:
Saransk
Project:
New stadium
Location:
Insar River basin
Home team:
FC Mordovia

DEVELOPMENT
Work on Mordovia Arena began in 2010, the 1,000th anniversary of the unification of the Mordovian people with Russia's other ethnic groups. The arena is located in the centre of the city, on the bank of the Insar River. The stadium will be home to FC Mordovia.

DESIGN
The stadium has been designed in the shape of an oval. Its bright range of colours, combining orange, red and white, honours the distinctive colour palette of Mordovia's arts and crafts.

CITY
Located in central Russia, Saransk is the capital of the Republic of Mordovia. It is one of the most pleasant cities in Russia, regularly scoring highly in the All-Russia city competition in recent years. Modern Mordovia carefully protects the unique languages and cultures of the Moksha and Erzya ethnic groups, who inhabited the area for centuries. Saransk is a frequent venue for ethnographic and folklore festivals aimed at preserving national identity, culture and customs.

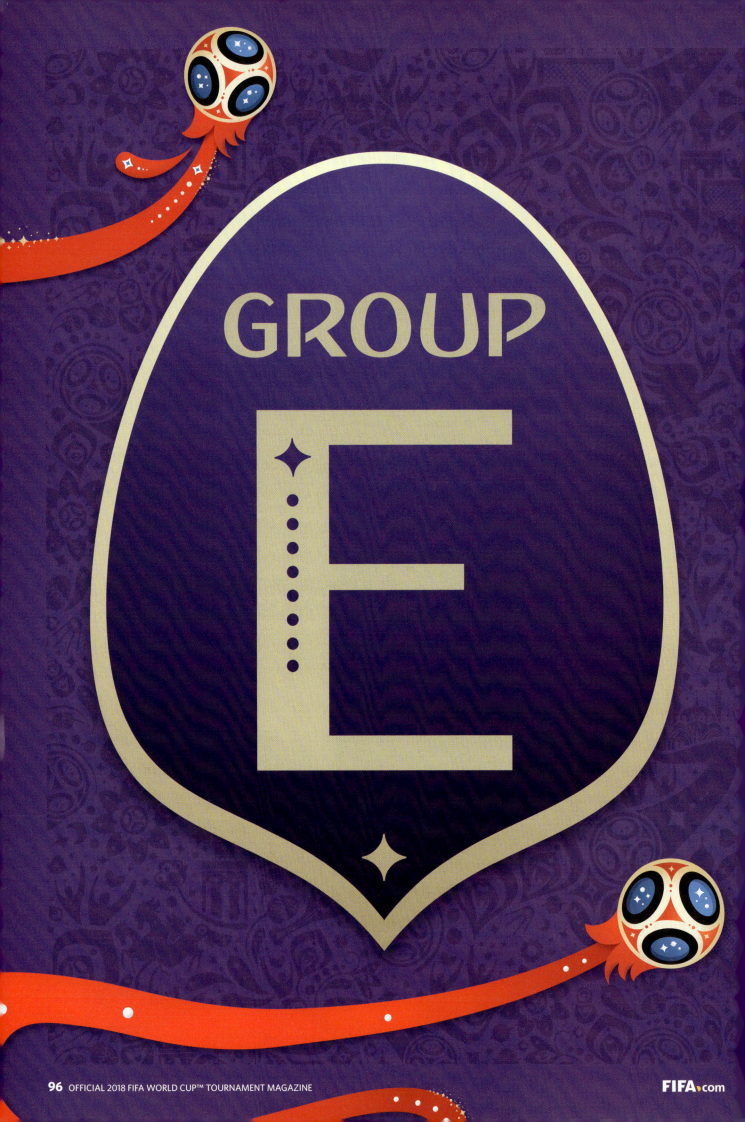

BRAZIL

SWITZERLAND

COSTA RICA

SERBIA

FIFA WORLD CUP RUSSIA 2018

Group E Fixtures

17 JUNE
Costa Rica v. Serbia
13:00
Samara Arena,
Samara

17 JUNE
Brazil v. Switzerland
19:00
Rostov Arena,
Rostov-on-Don

22 JUNE
Brazil v. Costa Rica
13:00
Saint Petersburg Stadium,
Saint Petersburg

22 JUNE
Serbia v. Switzerland
19:00
Kaliningrad Stadium,
Kaliningrad

27 JUNE
Serbia v. Brazil
19:00
Spartak Stadium,
Moscow

27 JUNE
Switzerland v. Costa Rica
19:00
Nizhny Novgorod Stadium,
Nizhny Novgorod

Kick-offs are UK time (UTC/GMT)

GROUP E

Brazil
Switzerland
Costa Rica
Serbia

BRAZIL

With five FIFA World Cup™ successes to their name, there is no doubt that Brazil are the first team on everybody's lips when it comes to discussing FIFA World Cup greats.

The entire history of the FIFA World Cup seems to be intertwined with the genius of the South American side and names such as Pelé, Cafu, Ronaldo, Ronaldinho, Kaká and Zico are among the most famous of all.

Hosting the tournament four years ago, Brazil's fans were left disappointed they could not win their first FIFA World Cup since 2002. However, recent success on home soil means hopes are again high that they can go all the way. At the 2016 Rio Olympics, Brazil did do enough to win the gold medal, beating Germany 5-4 on penalties in the final to offer a reminder to the rest of the world that they are always a strong team to face.

Brazil have been drawn in Group E, which will be a tough proposition as Switzerland, Costa Rica and Serbia will all be just as determined as Brazil to finish in first place and thus miss a potential round-of-16 match with defending champions Germany.

Although Brazil no longer possess a team based upon the sole genius of just one or two players, their attacking style and willingness to work harder together, aligned with their natural South American flair, will see them start the tournament as one of the favourites.

Nobody has won the FIFA World Cup as many times as Brazil but their fans are restless that their 16-year wait should come to an end.

Is 2018 FIFA World Cup Russia™ the time and place for Brazil to make it six successes? Only time will tell.

> "I think this World Cup is going to be huge for Brazilians. Personally, I'm going to give everything I've got to win it."
>
> — Neymar

HOW THEY QUALIFIED

While the likes of Argentina, Uruguay and Colombia had to endure some nerve-wracking moments in their last few qualifiers in order to feature at the 2018 FIFA World Cup in Russia, Brazil had no such concerns and coasted their way to the top of the South American qualifying group.

After a sluggish opening to their campaign, Tite became head coach in June 2016 and he inspired a wonderful Brazilian resurgence and the five-time winners became the first side to book their spot at the tournament in March 2017.

After 14 matches, they already had the necessary points margin to start finalising their Russian plans and they ended up topping their group with 12 wins from 18 matches, with five draws and just a solitary loss, to Chile in the opening match.

With 41 goals scored and just 11 conceded, Brazil were by far the superior side in their group and could afford to sit back and plan for Russia a long time ago.

Brazil
Switzerland
Costa Rica
Serbia

GROUP E

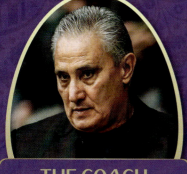

THE COACH

TITE

Since Tite became Brazil boss in June 2016, the side have not looked back and he took them on a nine-match winning streak in the group to easily qualify for the 2018 FIFA World Cup.

He won the FIFA Club World Cup 2012 title with Corinthians in Russia and is a widely respected coach in his homeland.

Although not as well-known as predecessors Dunga or Luiz Felipe Scolari, the way he now has Brazil firing proves he is the right man in the right place at the right time.

> "Individual talent is no longer enough on its own today. You need a whole series of factors to come together."

ALL-TIME TOP GOALSCORER
PELÉ
77

ALL-TIME MOST CAPS
CAFU
142

HAT-TRICK OF HEROES

PHILIPPE COUTINHO

The attacking midfielder became a firm fans' favourite in England after featuring for Premier League giants Liverpool from 2013 until his move to Barcelona in January.

Born and raised in Rio de Janeiro, Coutinho has skill and flair in abundance, an eye for goal and a willingness to track back and look for the ball.

He has an ability to score spectacular goals, has developed into something of a free-kick expert, and he was named in the 2014-15 Premier League Team of the Year.

His superb performances persuaded Barcelona to spend around £130million on him.

DANI ALVES

Dani Alves has played for clubs such as Sevilla, Barcelona, Juventus and Paris Saint-Germain and you do not get so many world-class clubs on your CV without being a special player.

The right back is equally classy going forward or defending and with six *La Liga* titles and one *Serie A* success to his name – as well as FIFA Confederation Cup victories in 2009 and 2013 – Alves has already tasted silverware success and will be keen for even more in Russia.

Not to be sniffed at either are the three UEFA Champions League winners' medals he collected with Barcelona and he is still performing to a very high level.

NEYMAR

When Neymar joined Paris Saint-Germain in 2017 for a record-breaking transfer fee, it still felt like great value for money, such is the forward's worth. The 26-year-old is as devastating a player as there is in world football.

Starting with Brazil side Santos in 2009 before moving to *La Liga* greats Barcelona four years later, Neymar's skills and ability on the ball won him fans across the globe.

Despite his tender years, he has already played nearly 90 times for his national side, underlining how highly he is regarded in his home country and a 2018 FIFA World Cup success would be just the next step along in a spectacular career.

FIFA World Cup™ Record

1930	GS	1958	C	1978	3rd	1998	RU
1934	R1	1962	C	1982	16	2002	C
1938	3rd	1966	GS	1986	QF	2006	QF
1950	RU	1970	C	1990	16	2010	QF
1954	QF	1974	4th	1994	C	2014	4th

DNE = Did not enter, **DNQ** = Did not qualify, **W** = Withdrew, **R1** = Round 1, **R2** = Round 2, **GS** = Group Stages, **16** = Last 16, **QF** = Quarter-finals, **4th** = Fourth place, **3rd** = Third place, **RU** = Runners-up, **C** = Champions

Statistics up until February 2018

GROUP E
Brazil
Switzerland
Costa Rica
Serbia

SWITZERLAND

Switzerland are one of the more experienced footballing nations at the 2018 FIFA World Cup™, this being the 11th time they have appeared in the finals.

Despite that impressive statistic, the Swiss only qualified for one FIFA World Cup™ between 1966 and 2006, that occasion coming in 1994.

Much of their FIFA World Cup success came in the early days of the competition, reaching the quarter-finals in 1934, 1938 and, as hosts, in 1954. In more recent times they have created FIFA World Cup history. In 2006 they reached the round of 16 before losing a shoot-out to the Ukraine and exited the tournament despite not having conceded a goal from play.

That 3-0 shoot-out defeat was also the first time a team had not managed to score during penalties in FIFA World Cup history.

At the following FIFA World Cup, they beat eventual champions Spain 1-0 in their opening group game and by the time Chile scored against them in the second match, they had set a FIFA World Cup record of 559 minutes without conceding a goal.

They failed to win their final group match and were eliminated but they qualified for the 2014 FIFA World Cup™, where a Xherdan Shaqiri hat-trick against Honduras ensured they progressed to the round of 16 before losing to Argentina.

Their record in the UEFA European Championships is more modest, having only qualified for four tournaments, but with talents like Shaqiri, Stephan Lichtsteiner and Breel Embolo to call upon, they will be looking to make a big impact in Russia.

> "It was very hard, there was a lot of pressure [in the play-off against Northern Ireland] but I'm very excited we've achieved our goal."
> — Yann Sommer

HOW THEY QUALIFIED

Switzerland executed an almost flawless qualifying campaign, yet still had to endure the tension of a play-off round to make it to Russia.

Their group fixtures handed them a very difficult start as they had to take on the newly-crowned European champions as Portugal came to St-Jakob Park in Basel.

However, goals from Breel Embolo and Admir Mehmedi gave the Swiss a 2-0 win and the best possible platform for a successful campaign.

Switzerland then rattled off eight more consecutive wins in a group also containing Hungary, Latvia, Faroe Islands and Andorra, and they went into the final group game – the return against Portugal – with a perfect record, but still needing a result to finish top of the group.

Portugal would win this time so the Swiss faced Northern Ireland in a play-off where a controversial penalty in the away leg was the only goal of the tie.

Brazil
Switzerland
Costa Rica
Serbia

GROUP **E**

FIFA WORLD CUP RUSSIA 2018

ALL-TIME TOP GOALSCORER
ALEXANDER FREI
42

ALL-TIME MOST CAPS
HEINZ HERMANN
118

THE COACH

VLADIMIR PETKOVIĆ

Vladimir Petković is a much-travelled and well-respected coach, who has been in charge of the Swiss national team since 2014.

His playing career as a midfielder saw him appear for many clubs – some of them more than once – in Switzerland, Bosnia, Slovenia and Serbia before he began his coaching career at Bellinzona, a club he represented four times as both a player and coach.

He went on to coach Lugano, Young Boys, Sion and Lazio, where he won the *Coppa Italia* in 2013, before taking over from Ottmar Hitzfeld with the Swiss national team after the 2014 FIFA World Cup in Brazil.

"Brazil are not the only opponents in the group, the others are also difficult. We must be prepared for Costa Rica, they are awkward opponents. Serbia have always had good individuals and this time they have formed a good group."

HAT-TRICK OF HEROES

STEPHAN LICHTSTEINER

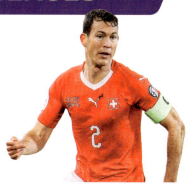

The attacking Swiss right back seems to have been around forever but that is because he consistently produces performances of such high quality.

He began his career with Grasshopper before a move to Lille in 2005. A year later he made his Switzerland debut against Brazil and has since had a 12-year international career which now sees him closing in on 100 caps.

Nicknamed Forrest Gump because of his lung-bursting runs down the right, he had a three-year spell with Lazio before moving to Juventus, where he has won numerous *Serie A* titles and appeared in a UEFA Champions League final.

BREEL EMBOLO

At the age of 21, Breel Embolo has already packed a lot into his short career and is one of the hottest prospects in European football.

Born in Cameroon, his mother brought him to Basel as a child, where he was picked up by the club's youth system, and just three weeks after his 16th birthday he signed his first professional contract.

He won three Swiss Super League medals before a big-money move to Schalke 04 in 2016.

He made his international debut against the United States not long after turning 18 with his biggest moment so far being when he scored against Portugal in a FIFA World Cup qualifier in 2016.

XHERDAN SHAQIRI

A true footballing star, Xherdan Shaqiri will be the man Swiss football fans look to to make things happen in Russia.

The stocky, skilful forward, who has played for Basel, Bayern Munich, Inter Milan, and now represents Stoke City, can operate across the front line or in a number 10 role and he has already had many big moments wearing his country's colours, including scoring two hat-tricks.

The first of those came in a 3-1 win over Bulgaria in UEFA EURO 2012 qualifying and the second earned a 3-0 victory over Honduras at the 2014 FIFA World Cup – the 50th hat-trick in FIFA World Cup history.

FIFA World Cup™ Record

1930	DNE	1958	DNQ	1978	DNQ	1998	DNQ
1934	QF	1962	GS	1982	DNQ	2002	DNQ
1938	QF	1966	GS	1986	DNQ	2006	16
1950	GS	1970	DNQ	1990	DNQ	2010	GS
1954	QF	1974	DNQ	1994	16	2014	16

DNE = Did not enter, **DNQ** = Did not qualify, **W** = Withdrew, **R1** = Round 1, **R2** = Round 2, **GS** = Group Stages, **16** = Last 16, **QF** = Quarter-finals, **4th** = Fourth place, **3rd** = Third place, **RU** = Runners-up, **C** = Champions

Statistics up until February 2018

GROUP **E**

Brazil
Switzerland
Costa Rica
Serbia

COSTA RICA

When the draw for Group E at the 2018 FIFA World Cup™ was made, some observers would have assumed that Costa Rica would be intimidated by being placed in the same group as Brazil, Serbia and Switzerland. After all, they are three countries with very strong footballing pedigrees and passions.

But underestimating Costa Rica has proven to be a very foolish prospect in the past – and could be again in Russia.

At the 2014 FIFA World Cup™, Costa Rica appeared to have an impossible task on their hands if they wanted to progress beyond the group stage as they were placed with three former world champions; Italy, Uruguay and England.

Yet rather than view their task as being insurmountable, Costa Rica won two matches and drew the third to wonderfully qualify for the round of 16.

After beating Greece 5-3 on penalties following a 1-1 draw, Costa Rica then lost in the quarter-finals on penalties to the highly regarded Netherlands.

Although they went home with tears in their eyes, they had at least shown the world that they were now a force to be reckoned with and that anybody underestimating them did so at their peril.

The fearlessness, direct style of play and hard work that brought Costa Rica such success four years ago will be more than evident again at the 2018 FIFA World Cup and manager Óscar Ramírez has moulded a team that could again upset some big opponents.

> "National hero? I don't know; what I know is that I get in the history of Costa Rica."
> — Kendall Waston

HOW THEY QUALIFIED

Costa Rica qualified for the 2018 FIFA World Cup with a match to spare and joined Mexico as CONCACAF's second qualified nation in round 5 as they drew 1-1 with Honduras in October 2017.

In San Jose, Honduras took the lead after 66 minutes when Eddie Hernández scored a fine header, but one of Costa Rica's best traits is their togetherness and they threw everything at Honduras until Kendall Waston scored in the fifth minute of stoppage time to earn Costa Rica the point they needed to make it to Russia.

The crucial match was actually played a day later than was originally scheduled due to a tropical storm but Costa Rica shrugged off the delay, rolled up their sleeves and booked their place at the 2018 FIFA World Cup.

In all their group matches, Costa Rica played ten games, winning four, drawing four and losing the remaining two and their strong defensive performance across those matches – conceding just eight times – was key to their success.

Brazil
Switzerland
Costa Rica
Serbia

GROUP **E**

FIFA WORLD CUP RUSSIA 2018

ALL-TIME TOP GOALSCORER
ROLANDO FONSECA
47

ALL-TIME MOST CAPS
WALTER CENTENO
137

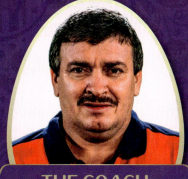

THE COACH

ÓSCAR RAMÍREZ

Óscar Ramírez is a man who has Costa Rican football in his heart and soul.

The 53-year-old represented his country 75 times over a 12-year period from 1985-1997 and he is now in charge of the side and loving every minute of it.

After great domestic success at Alajuelense, he became national coach in 2015, replacing Paulo Wanchope, and he has done a brilliant job in squeezing every ounce of talent from the players at his disposal.

One thing is for certain in Russia: Costa Rica will fear no opponent and they will play with a style that will make them a joy to watch.

"History tells us that whenever we've faced European teams, we've always kicked on and had our best World Cups ever. After what happened in 2014 we're not really scared of anyone."

HAT-TRICK OF HEROES

KENDALL WASTON

Kendall Waston is a very tall and very tough defender who features for Vancouver Whitecaps domestically and who scored the crucial goal that helped Costa Rica plan for the 2018 FIFA World Cup in Russia.

The ecstatic way he celebrated his header against Honduras with his team-mates showed how important the national side is to him and he has a very dangerous knack of scoring headers from set-pieces that Costa Rica's opponents should be wary of.

In fact, Waston scored two goals in qualifying and both came in 1-1 draws with the Hondurans.

BRYAN RUIZ

Bryan Ruiz has been a class act in European football for over a decade having joined Gent from Alajuelense in 2006.

He has gone on to play for FC Twente, Fulham, PSV Eindhoven and Sporting Lisbon and all of those clubs have benefitted from his attacking mindset, eye for goal and ability to make opportunities for other players.

At 32, this may be his last FIFA World Cup™ but he is certainly aiming to leave his mark on the tournament and Costa Rica will desperately hope he is at his very best in Russia.

KEYLOR NAVAS

Keylor Navas is a very safe option between the posts for Costa Rica and has performed at a consistently high level for many a season.

You do not become a formidable presence at a club the size of Real Madrid unless you are a very astute, intelligent and athletic footballer and Navas certainly ticks all of the boxes for both club and country.

Navas was the man of the match for Costa Rica against Greece at the 2014 FIFA World Cup after a series of wonderful saves and finished the tournament as one of the nominees for the Golden Glove Award for best goalkeeper.

FIFA World Cup™ Record

1930	DNE	1958	DNQ	1978	DNQ	1998	DNQ
1934	DNE	1962	DNQ	1982	DNQ	2002	GS
1938	DNE	1966	DNQ	1986	DNQ	2006	GS
1950	DNE	1970	DNQ	1990	16	2010	DNQ
1954	DNE	1974	DNQ	1994	DNQ	2014	QF

DNE = Did not enter, **DNQ** = Did not qualify, **W** = Withdrew, **R1** = Round 1, **R2** = Round 2, **GS** = Group Stages, **16** = Last 16, **QF** = Quarter-finals, **4th** = Fourth place, **3rd** = Third place, **RU** = Runners-up, **C** = Champions

Statistics up until February 2018

GROUP E
Brazil
Switzerland
Costa Rica
Serbia

SERBIA

Serbia's wait for a return to football's top table is over – and the entire country is rejoicing.

Eastern Europe is a renowned hotbed for sporting passion but few countries can claim to be as football-mad as Serbia and after failing to qualify for the 2014 FIFA World Cup™, the glee with which their presence in Russia will be felt across the nation is palpable.

After years of political unrest as part of Yugoslavia and then Serbia and Montenegro, Serbia first competed as an independent footballing nation at the 2010 FIFA World Cup™ and the sense of pride felt by that team – managed by Radomir Antić – is still evident in its current crop of players.

Serbia have a proud heritage and some of their former players such as Dejan Stanković and Nemanja Vidić are heralded as legends in their homeland. It is time for a new brand of Serbian superstar to emerge at the 2018 FIFA World Cup™ and players such Aleksandar Kolarov, Aleksandar Mitrović and Mijat Gaćinović all have the opportunity to cement their names in Serbian sporting folklore.

Serbia's build-up to the 2018 FIFA World Cup has hardly been ideal after replacing Slavoljub Muslin with Mladen Krstajić as head coach in the run-up to the tournament.

However, one of Serbian football's biggest and strongest traits is the team spirit and patriotism that oozes from the squad.

> "Serbia is a small country. It would be unrealistic to suggest that we'll win the World Cup, but we'll never give up – this is our mentality. We'll try to take every opportunity we get. We'll fight until the end!"
>
> — Branislav Ivanović

HOW THEY QUALIFIED

Serbia made their way to Russia thanks to topping qualifying Group D back in October last year.

After beating Georgia 1-0 at home courtesy of an Aleksandar Prijović goal, that was enough for Serbia to fend off the Republic of Ireland's chase and finish Group D on 21 points from their ten matches, two points ahead of second place.

Of those encounters, they won six, drew three and lost just one match – a 3-2 defeat to Austria on October 6.

The goals of Aleksandar Mitrović, with six strikes, and Dušan Tadić, with four, were the crucial difference for Serbia in a hard-fought, competitive group that ebbed and flowed throughout.

Only six points separated the top four sides but the fact Serbia scored 20 goals in their ten matches – eight more than second-placed Ireland – and finished with a goal difference of +10 shows they can be a real attacking force on their day.

Brazil
Switzerland
Costa Rica
Serbia

GROUP **E**

FIFA WORLD CUP RUSSIA 2018

THE COACH

ALL-TIME TOP GOALSCORER
STJEPAN BOBEK
38

ALL-TIME MOST CAPS
DEJAN STANKOVIĆ
103

HAT-TRICK OF HEROES

MLADEN KRSTAJIĆ

Mladen Krstajić will be pinching himself when he leads Serbia out at the 2018 FIFA World Cup.

Former Serbia manager Slavoljub Muslin led the country to Russia but he was sacked in October 2017 and Krstajić – who played for Werder Bremen, Schalke 04 and FK Partizan – was appointed caretaker manager for a two-month period before being named full-time manager in December last year.

The former Yugoslavia defender impressed during his interim period in charge and knows he has the chance to live the dream as manager of the Serbian national side on the biggest stage of all.

ALEKSANDAR KOLAROV

Roma defender Aleksandar Kolarov is renowned for his athleticism, competitive nature and versatility and his experience will be crucial for Serbia if they are to shine in Russia.

After beginning his career at Čukarički, the 32-year-old moved to OFK Beograd and Lazio before enjoying a brilliantly successful seven-season spell at Manchester City in the Premier League.

He is equally comfortable at either left back or in central defence and he is also a very dangerous dead-ball striker, using his hammer of a left foot to great effect, and was named as Serbia's player of the year in 2011.

ALEKSANDAR MITROVIĆ

Aleksandar Mitrović is a Newcastle United striker who is only just starting out on a career that seems full to the brim with talent and promise.

He made his breakthrough with Partizan, became well-known at Anderlecht and then moved to Newcastle, although he spent some of last season on loan to Fulham.

Mitrović is a tall, strong and imposing striker who likes the ball at his feet.

At the 2013 European Under-19 Championship he was one of the truly standout performers and he has since gone on to be equally impressive for the full Serbian side as well.

"The young and upcoming players in the squad are Serbia's future and they will get a chance to prove their worth as well as to show what they can bring into the World Cup roster."

NEMANJA MATIĆ

Nemanja Matić is one of the crucial cogs in a team's machine that every club wishes they could call their own.

The 29-year-old is a defensive midfielder but he actually began his career as somebody more interested in going forward and that is still visible in his style of play as he likes to get into the opposition's half when the time is right.

Manchester United manager José Mourinho brought him to Old Trafford last year after three successful years at Chelsea and the tall, tough midfielder has many good seasons ahead of him.

Serbia is deemed the direct successor to both SFR Yugoslavia and Serbia and Montenegro by FIFA, and therefore the inheritor to all the records of the defunct nations

FIFA World Cup™ Record

1930	4th	1958	QF	1978	DNQ	1998	16
1934	DNQ	1962	4th	1982	GS	2002	DNQ
1938	DNQ	1966	DNQ	1986	DNQ	2006	GS
1950	GS	1970	DNQ	1990	QF	2010	GS
1954	QF	1974	16	1994	DNE	2014	DNQ

DNE = Did not enter, **DNQ** = Did not qualify, **W** = Withdrew, **R1** = Round 1, **R2** = Round 2, **GS** = Group Stages, **16** = Last 16, **QF** = Quarter-finals, **4th** = Fourth place, **3rd** = Third place, **RU** = Runners-up, **C** = Champions

Statistics up until February 2018

GERMANY

MEXICO

SWEDEN

KFA

KOREA REPUBLIC

Group F Fixtures

17 JUNE
Germany v. Mexico
16:00
Luzhniki Stadium,
Moscow

18 JUNE
Sweden v. Korea Republic
13:00
Nizhny Novgorod Stadium,
Nizhny Novgorod

23 JUNE
Korea Republic v. Mexico
16:00
Rostov Arena,
Rostov-on-Don

23 JUNE
Germany v. Sweden
19:00
Fisht Stadium,
Sochi

27 JUNE
Korea Republic v. Germany
15:00
Kazan Arena,
Kazan

27 JUNE
Mexico v. Sweden
15:00
Ekaterinburg Arena,
Ekaterinburg

Kick-offs are UK time (UTC/GMT)

GROUP F
Germany
Mexico
Sweden
Korea Republic

GERMANY

There are successful footballing nations, there are superb footballing nations and then there is international footballing royalty.

There is no doubt whatsoever which category Germany belong in. Having won the FIFA World Cup™ an astonishing four times and also been runners-up on a further four occasions, there is no doubt that they have historically been one of the world's most spectacular footballing forces.

The ingredients for a successful German side appear to have remained unchanged throughout the decades. A combination of outstanding fitness and teamwork is aligned with flashes of genius.

The Germany side has always possessed plenty of pride and a high work ethic and they remain ice-cool when the heat is on.

Manager Joachim Löw was in charge four years ago when Germany lifted the official trophy in Brazil and he must be quietly confident that he can lead Germany to more glory in Russia and become the first side since Brazil in 1962 to retain the FIFA World Cup.

And, of course, they have already tasted success on Russian soil after winning the FIFA Confederations Cup 2017.

Germany play an unfussy brand of football that provides results. To them, winning in knockout football is all that matters.

While absolutely nothing is guaranteed in the constantly changing world of football, what is almost certain is that Germany will be in the hunt for a fifth FIFA World Cup win in Russia.

> "A good team spirit and gameplan can be decisive in beating teams that are stronger man for man. If you don't play as a unit, it makes life incredibly difficult against any side."
> — Benedikt Höwedes

HOW THEY QUALIFIED

It is rare that any side can say they cruised to qualification for a FIFA World Cup – the prize at stake makes easy matches few and far between – but Germany can certainly claim to have enjoyed their progress towards Russia more than most.

In Group C, they easily topped the group with second-placed Northern Ireland falling 11 points short of Germany's flawless tally of 30.

Perhaps the highlight of their ten games was the 6-0 home victory over Norway, having already beaten the Scandinavians 3-0 away. Indeed, only one of their wins was by a single goal.

What was most impressive was both Germany's attacking and defensive prowess. They scored an incredible 43 goals in their ten qualifying matches and conceded on just four occasions.

That is a stunning statistic that demonstrates their strength in depth all over the pitch and the threat they pose to the other fancied teams in Russia.

Germany
Mexico
Sweden
Korea Republic

GROUP F

THE COACH

JOACHIM LÖW

Joachim Löw took over as manager of the German national side in 2006 after over a decade of experience in domestic management.

The former attacking midfielder has taken that ethos with him into his managerial career and his Germany side loves to get forward at every opportunity.

One of his key ideas is to get the ball passed from player to player as quickly as possible.

Reaching the final of UEFA EURO 2008 underlined his ability to take sides to the latter stages of major tournaments and this was best proven four years ago when Löw's men crushed Brazil 7-1 in their 2014 FIFA World Cup™ semi-final on their way to a hard-fought final victory over Argentina.

"We are the defending world champions, we have won the Confederations Cup, our goal can only be to stay on top, but that'll be difficult. We have won it all lately and everybody wants to beat us."

ALL-TIME TOP GOALSCORER
MIROSLAV KLOSE
71

ALL-TIME MOST CAPS
LOTHAR MATTHÄUS
150

HAT-TRICK OF HEROES

SAMI KHEDIRA

Midfielder Sami Khedira has played over 70 matches for Germany and has become increasingly influential.

He is a good leader – indeed, he has captained Germany several times – and his ability to get the best from those around him is seen as one of his biggest assets.

Khedira's career began at VfB Stuttgart and he moved on to the mighty Real Madrid but he has really blossomed in *Serie A* with Juventus.

He is one of a group of experienced German midfielders who have grown together and will be at their peak in the summer of 2018.

MESUT ÖZIL

Mesut Özil's value to Germany can be proven by the fact he's won 29 out of 34 matches played in FIFA tournaments.

The Arsenal playmaker is a stunningly talented player on the ball and as he nears a century of caps for his national team, he will be hoping to continue his fine run of form in Russia.

He is a Rolls-Royce of a player who glides gracefully over the grass and can strike a ball with pace and accuracy with that wand of a left foot.

At 29 years of age, Özil is in the prime of his career, has been in great form and could really hurt Germany's opponents this summer.

TONI KROOS

Toni Kroos is a mainstay of Real Madrid's midfield and you have to be a particularly talented footballer to be able to claim that position.

A winner of countless team and individual honours – including two UEFA Champions League medals – he started his career with Bayern Munich.

The 28-year-old has played for Germany since 2010 and he has been an integral member of Joachim Löw's squad.

He is widely considered to be one of the best attacking midfielders in the world and he is well on course to win over 100 caps for his country in the coming seasons.

FIFA World Cup™ Record

1930	DNE	1958	4th	1978	16	1998	QF
1934	3rd	1962	QF	1982	RU	2002	RU
1938	GS	1966	RU	1986	RU	2006	3rd
1950	W	1970	3rd	1990	C	2010	3rd
1954	C	1974	C	1994	QF	2014	C

DNE = Did not enter, **DNQ** = Did not qualify, **W** = Withdrew, **R1** = Round 1, **R2** = Round 2, **GS** = Group Stages, **16** = Last 16, **QF** = Quarter-finals, **4th** = Fourth place, **3rd** = Third place, **RU** = Runners-up, **C** = Champions

Statistics up until February 2018

GROUP F
Germany
Mexico
Sweden
Korea Republic

MEXICO

By blending the old(er) with the new, Mexico are hoping to finally climb over the round-of-16 summit and progress to the higher ground of the quarter-finals at the 2018 FIFA World Cup™.

Mexico possesses a fine FIFA World Cup™ pedigree, having qualified for 15 editions of the tournament, but in recent times they have always come unstuck at the round-of-16 stage. In fact, Mexico have to look back to the golden year of the 1986 FIFA World Cup™ – which they themselves hosted – in order to remember the last time they made the last eight of the tournament.

Six consecutive FIFA World Cup™ editions of failing at the round-of-16 stage has made the country more focused than ever on going at least one step further.

The good news for fans of *El Tri* is that they arguably have the best chance ever. Manager Juan Carlos Osorio has worked hard at using both more experienced players such as Javier "Chicharito" Hernández alongside exciting young guns in the form of Hirving Lozano and they are expected to seize their opportunity to show the world how good Mexico can be.

Led by the experienced team captain Andrés Guardado, Mexico are in a difficult group alongside Germany, Sweden and Korea Republic, yet they have plenty of international class and experience and plenty of desire to push favourites Germany all the way.

Only time will tell if Mexico can replicate their 1986 FIFA World Cup success of reaching deep into the tournament.

> "I'm proud to have a shot at a fourth World Cup. Most importantly, it's my last chance to be part of a team that goes down in Mexican football history."
> — Andrés Guardado

HOW THEY QUALIFIED

Mexico were simply brilliant in qualifying for the 2018 FIFA World Cup as they won CONCACAF Group A in round 4 of qualifying, winning five of their six matches to beat Honduras to first place with 16 points, before showing equally impressive form in round 5.

After ten matches they had scored 16 goals – the second highest in the group – but had, crucially, conceded on just seven occasions.

That miserly defence was the foundation for their successful campaign and by winning six of their ten matches, Mexico finished ahead of Costa Rica as round 5 winners with an impressive 21 points, five more than Costa Rica.

An impressive 1-0 win over the USA in November 2016 set the tone for the rest of the group and Mexico suffered just one loss, a 3-2 defeat to Honduras in their last qualifier when they had already sealed their passage to Russia.

Germany
Mexico
Sweden
Korea Republic

GROUP **F**

THE COACH

JUAN CARLOS OSORIO

Colombian Juan Carlos Osorio is a figure who divides opinion in Mexico but there is little doubt that his obsessive training methods are paying dividends for *El Tri*.

Osorio is perhaps the most intense coach in world football and he spends hours poring over tactics, training schedules and different routines in order to get the best from his squad.

He also frequently travels the world to watch other coaches in action and has recently observed both Brendan Rodgers at Celtic and also Jorge Sampaoli when he was at Sevilla.

Osorio demands the best from his squad and is also determined to help them progress further than the round of 16 – the stage where Mexico tend to falter at the FIFA World Cup.

> "The players have come to understand that if we are going to improve, we have to improve in every way collectively. We really think that we are no longer a group of good players. We are a proper team now."

ALL-TIME TOP GOALSCORER
JAVIER HERNÁNDEZ
49

ALL-TIME MOST CAPS
CLAUDIO SUÁREZ
177

HAT-TRICK OF HEROES

JAVIER HERNÁNDEZ

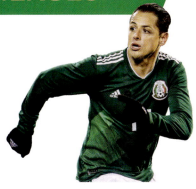

Javier "Chicharito" Hernández is a hero in his homeland for his eye for goal and he is already Mexico's all-time leading goalscorer at 29 years of age.

Plucked from Guadalajara by Sir Alex Ferguson at Manchester United, Hernández displayed an uncanny eye for goal at Old Trafford for five seasons between 2010 and 2015 before spells at Real Madrid and Bayer Leverkusen followed ahead of a return to the Premier League at West Ham United.

Fiercely committed to the Mexican cause, Hernández has become a master at unlocking defences and he will be going all out to help Mexico progress in Russia.

GUILLERMO OCHOA

Guillermo Ochoa has played for Mexico since 2005 and there are no signs that he will stop any time soon.

The 32-year-old has played nearly 100 times for Mexico – and has previously been to three FIFA World Cups – and plays for Standard Liège in Belgium, where he is as highly regarded as he is in his home country.

Ochoa is not particularly tall for a goalkeeper but what the former Ajaccio and Málaga man lacks in height he makes up for in presence, intelligence and sharp decision-making.

Curiously, he plays with the number 13 on his back as his birthday is 13 July.

HECTOR MORENO

Hector Moreno is a 30-year-old central defender who is coming into his own as a leader and as a footballer.

The Roma player has enjoyed a fruitful career in Europe, featuring for sides such as AZ, Espanyol and PSV, and he is on course to play for his national side for many years to come.

He has featured in two previous FIFA World Cup editions, in 2010 and 2014, and he certainly has the experience, know-how and desire to help *El Tri* prosper in Russia.

Moreno likes the physical side of the game and is also a decisive and influential passer of the ball.

FIFA World Cup™ Record

1930	GS	1958	GS	1978	GS	1998	16
1934	DNQ	1962	GS	1982	DNQ	2002	16
1938	W	1966	GS	1986	QF	2006	16
1950	GS	1970	QF	1990	Banned	2010	16
1954	GS	1974	DNQ	1994	16	2014	16

DNE = Did not enter, **DNQ** = Did not qualify, **W** = Withdrew, **R1** = Round 1, **R2** = Round 2, **GS** = Group Stages, **16** = Last 16, **QF** = Quarter-finals, **4th** = Fourth place, **3rd** = Third place, **RU** = Runners-up, **C** = Champions

Statistics up until February 2018

GROUP **F** — Germany, Mexico, **Sweden**, Korea Republic

SWEDEN

After stunning four-time FIFA World Cup™ winners Italy in the play-offs to reach their 12th finals, Sweden will be confident of causing more upsets in Russia – in what will be their first FIFA World Cup tournament since the last European edition of the competition, in 2006.

Historically one of the stronger European nations in FIFA World Cup history, Janne Andersson's squad will believe they have enough quality to overcome the challenge of Mexico and Korea Republic to qualify for the knockout phase, with FIFA World Cup holders Germany the standout nation in Group F.

A team reliant on organisation and hard work rather than individual talent, one conundrum to consider in the lead-up to the tournament will be whether to lure all-time record goalscorer Zlatan Ibrahimović out of international retirement and risk disrupting the system which has helped the nation reach the finals.

Sweden's best FIFA World Cup™ performance came 60 years ago when they were hosts. It is a tournament that has gone down in football history courtesy of Brazil's first victory, defeating the home side 5-2 when they featured a 17-year-old by the name of Pelé.

In more modern times, third place was achieved in the USA in 1994, when the likes of goalkeeper Thomas Ravelli and forwards Martin Dahlin, Tomas Brolin and Kennet Andersson wrote themselves into Swedish football history. What chance the class of 2018 achieving something similar?

> "I'm so proud of us. We have believed in this, we know how strong we are. I think that's the key – we know how strong we are. We help each other in every situation."
> — Marcus Berg

HOW THEY QUALIFIED

Sweden reached their 12th FIFA World Cup by defeating seeded Italy 1-0 on aggregate in a play-off, holding the *Azzurri* to a goalless draw in the second leg in Milan.

Jakob Johansson proved the hero, his winner in the first leg – his first international goal – in Stockholm proving decisive against arguably the toughest opposition they could have drawn.

They had done well just to reach that stage, having been put in pot three in a qualification group that included top-seeded Netherlands and 1998 FIFA World Cup™ champions France, who were in pot two and had reached the final of UEFA EURO 2016.

The French finished top with Sweden as runners-up, being Group A's highest scorers thanks to crushing wins home and away over Belarus, and a record 8-0 triumph over Luxembourg. The goals helped push the Netherlands into third thanks to goal difference.

A 2-1 comeback victory over France proved key midway through the qualification campaign.

Germany
Mexico
Sweden
Korea Republic

GROUP F

THE COACH

ALL-TIME TOP GOALSCORER
ZLATAN IBRAHIMOVIĆ
62

ALL-TIME MOST CAPS
ANDERS SVENSSON
148

HAT-TRICK OF HEROES

ANDREAS GRANQVIST

Captain for club and country, key central defender Andreas Granqvist has been a mainstay of Krasnodar's backline since summer 2013, helping the Russian side establish themselves as one of the top-five clubs in the country, as well as guiding them into European competition for the first time.

Successor to Ibrahimović as skipper following his international retirement post-UEFA EURO 2016, he also followed Ibra as Swedish Player of the Year – the first player other than Ibra to win it since 2006.

As well as Krasnodar, Granqvist's career has taken him to Helsingborgs, Wigan Athletic, Groningen and Genoa.

JANNE ANDERSON

Janne Andersson is one of the most respected coaches in the Swedish game, having made headlines after guiding unfashionable IFK Norrköping to their first league title for 26 years in 2015.

Inspired by Bengt Johansson, a former handball coach who served as his primary school sports teacher in his home neighbourhood of Halmstad, an undistinguished playing career was spent mainly at local side Alets IK, with whom he enjoyed two spells, before moving into coaching with the club, in 1988.

He also coached at Halmstads BK and Örgryte before making his name with IFK, with whom he also won the Swedish Super Cup. He has helped lift the nation in the wake of Ibrahimović's retirement and exit in the group phase at UEFA EURO 2016, with the squad's collective strength proving key in view of the dearth of individual world-class talent in the squad.

MIKAEL LUSTIG

The right-sided defender is preparing for his third major tournament, having played in the last two European Championships.

Having scored three times in qualifying, Lustig will expect to have wrapped up a seventh successive Scottish Premiership title with Celtic by the time the finals begin, having passed 200 appearances for the club in 2017/18.

Lustig made his debut for Sweden in 2008 against the USA, while his first international goal came against Moldova in 2011.

He scored a big goal in Sweden's qualification campaign, netting the winner in a 1-0 away victory against Luxembourg.

> "Look at some of the older players who felt that this was the last chance to make it to a World Cup – and now we did it. It's indescribable."

MARCUS BERG

Plying his trade with Al Ain in the UAE, the striker was Sweden's star performer in qualifying, netting eight times including four in the 8-0 defeat of Luxembourg, the country's biggest win in 79 years.

Having scored nearly 100 goals in four seasons with Panathinaikos, Berg has continued that scoring form with his new club, who were among the title contenders in 2017/18.

Aged 31, Berg has enough experience and ability to deal with the pressure of trying to fill the sizeable goalscoring boots of the retired Zlatan Ibrahimović.

FIFA World Cup™ Record

1930	DNE	1958	RU	1978	GS	1998	DNQ
1934	QF	1962	DNQ	1982	DNQ	2002	16
1938	4th	1966	DNQ	1986	DNQ	2006	16
1950	3rd	1970	GS	1990	GS	2010	DNQ
1954	DNQ	1974	R2	1994	3rd	2014	DNQ

DNE = Did not enter, **DNQ** = Did not qualify, **W** = Withdrew, **R1** = Round 1, **R2** = Round 2, **GS** = Group Stages, **16** = Last 16, **QF** = Quarter-finals, **4th** = Fourth place, **3rd** = Third place, **RU** = Runners-up, **C** = Champions

Statistics up until February 2018

GROUP F
Germany
Mexico
Sweden
Korea Republic

KOREA REPUBLIC

If you want to see the best Asian team in the history of the FIFA World Cup™ then look no further than Korea Republic.

The *Taegeuk Warriors* may not have inspired much on their long and arduous qualification journey to Russia but the fact they are at the tournament itself should surprise nobody.

Put simply, no Asian country has ever been as consistent as Korea Republic when it comes to qualifying.

It was not always that way. The early years of FIFA World Cup did not contain Korea Republic for a variety of reasons, although they did get to the 1954 edition.

There was then another huge wait until 1986 – but since then, they have not looked back and they have featured in nine consecutive tournaments, a feat that deserves to be acknowledged.

How well Korea Republic do in Russia remains to be seen but they have plenty of pace and wizardry going forward and if they can click under relatively new manager Shin Tae-yong then Korea Republic will he hoping to emulate their achievements of 2002, when they finished fourth on home soil.

That tournament really ignited Korea Republic's love of football and many of those doing battle in Russia will have been inspired by their heroes from 16 years ago.

Now is the time for Korea Republic to find new heroes and prove that not only are they consistent FIFA World Cup qualifiers but that they can also produce when it matters the most.

> "Like any other players from throughout the world, we see qualification to the World Cup as the most important achievement. It is a dream we have had since childhood."
>
> — Jung Woo-young

HOW THEY QUALIFIED

Despite being widely tipped as the strongest team in Group A – which also included IR Iran, Syria, Uzbekistan, China PR and Qatar – Korea Republic failed to sparkle like they quite expected to in the crucial third round of Asian qualifying.

They made heavy weather of making it to Russia and of their ten group encounters, they won just four, drew a further three and then lost the remaining three.

In a low-scoring group, they actually scored the most goals with 11 but they also conceded ten, which meant qualification for Russia was never a foregone conclusion.

Indeed, it was actually IR Iran who won the group on 22 points, a full seven ahead of Korea Republic. With two places in Russia up for grabs, Shin Tae-yong's side finished second, two points ahead of Syria and Uzbekistan.

When all is said and done, the *Taegeuk Warriors* did enough to qualify for the 2018 FIFA World Cup™ and they will not look back now.

Germany
Mexico
Sweden
Korea Republic

GROUP **F**

THE COACH

ALL-TIME TOP GOALSCORER
CHA BUM-KUN
57

ALL-TIME MOST CAPS
HONG MYUNG-BO
136

HAT-TRICK OF HEROES

SON HEUNG-MIN
Son Heung-min is probably the best known Korea Republic player because of the talents he has displayed at Tottenham Hotspur in the Premier League in recent times.

Son has a wonderful touch, he can spot a seemingly impossible pass and he also likes to score himself.

Harry Kane may have taken a lot of the plaudits for Tottenham's current attacking prowess but Son deserves a chunk of credit too and he will certainly get the chance in Russia to show he is at the very top of his game.

Son has played for his national team since 2010 and is one of his country's leading lights.

KI SUNG-YUENG
Central midfielder and Korea Republic captain Ki Sung-yueng plies his trade at Swansea City and the 29-year-old has become renowned for his superb passing consistency and range of skills, and although Swansea City have struggled to dominate in the English game recently, Ki has been an influential performer.

The former Celtic star is equally comfortable delivering crosses from dead-ball situations or while running at pace and his long-range passing is particularly noteworthy.

Russia will be the perfect stage to showcase his skills and Korea Republic will look to him to provide plenty of chances.

LEE CHUNG-YONG
Lee Chung-yong was one of Korea Republic's breakthrough Premier League names when he flew to England to join Bolton Wanderers from FC Seoul back in 2009 and his electric pace and ability to provide intelligent crosses proved that he was more than capable of producing the goods in the English top-flight.

Since then he has moved to Crystal Palace but his qualities, his vision and his professionalism remain exactly the same.

He is a very dangerous opponent on his day and his ability to twist and turn his way into the penalty area should not be underestimated.

SHIN TAE-YONG
Shin Tae-yong was a deputy of former manager Uli Stielike but was drafted in for Korea Republic's last two qualifying matches after a series of results and performances that failed to inspire.

Originally his contract only extended until the end of the qualification stage but back-to-back goalless draws in the matches he oversaw – against IR Iran and Uzbekistan respectively – helped book Korea Republic's place.

It was not that pretty but it was certainly effective and Tae-yong now has to prove he has galvanised his young squad sufficiently, something that might come easy to a man nicknamed the "Asian Mourinho".

"We will prepare for the World Cup thoroughly. I'm a man who likes to play attacking football. People will find out about South Korea's true football power at the World Cup."

FIFA World Cup™ Record

1930	DNE	1958	DNE	1978	DNQ	1998	GS
1934	DNE	1962	DNQ	1982	DNQ	2002	4th
1938	DNE	1966	DNE	1986	GS	2006	GS
1950	DNE	1970	DNQ	1990	GS	2010	16
1954	GS	1974	DNQ	1994	GS	2014	GS

DNE = Did not enter, **DNQ** = Did not qualify, **W** = Withdrew, **R1** = Round 1, **R2** = Round 2, **GS** = Group Stages, **16** = Last 16, **QF** = Quarter-finals, **4th** = Fourth place, **3rd** = Third place, **RU** = Runners-up, **C** = Champions

Statistics up until February 2018

First of many...

Goalscorer Vavá and Pelé embrace after Brazil went 2-1 up in the final of the 1958 FIFA World Cup™ in Solna, near Stockholm. Both players scored twice in a 5-2 win that saw the Brazilians claim their first title. Swedish goalkeeper Karl Svensson can't hide his disappointment. Pelé ultimately played a part in three Brazil FIFA World Cup™ wins while his country has claimed five titles in all.

BELGIUM

PANAMA

TUNISIA

ENGLAND

FIFA WORLD CUP RUSSIA 2018

Group G Fixtures

18 JUNE
Belgium v. Panama
16:00
Fisht Stadium, Sochi

18 JUNE
Tunisia v. England
19:00
Volgograd Arena, Volgograd

23 JUNE
Belgium v. Tunisia
13:00
Spartak Stadium, Moscow

24 JUNE
England v. Panama
13:00
Nizhny Novgorod Stadium, Nizhny Novgorod

28 JUNE
England v. Belgium
19:00
Kaliningrad Stadium, Kaliningrad

28 JUNE
Panama v. Tunisia
19:00
Mordovia Arena, Saransk

Kick-offs are UK time (UTC/GMT)

GROUP G
- Belgium
- Panama
- Tunisia
- England

BELGIUM

For many a decade, fans of Belgium have been wondering exactly when their country's football team would begin to fulfil its undoubted vast potential.

And the answer could well be: the 2018 FIFA World Cup Russia™.

Looking at the Belgium side on paper is to look at a team oozing with brilliant performers all over the field and if they all hit peak form at the same time, then anything could happen in Russia.

Names such as Romelu Lukaku, Kevin De Bruyne, Jan Vertonghen, Radja Nainggolan, Toby Alderweireld and Vincent Kompany deserve to be talked about in the highest possible terms and it is now the job of manager Roberto Martínez to ensure they gel properly in Russia. The former Everton manager has certainly united his squad and will look to build upon Belgium's showing at the last FIFA World Cup™.

Four years ago, Belgium got to the quarter-finals in Brazil, their best performance at a FIFA World Cup since they finished fourth in 1986, but even that felt as if they had fallen short and that the country's brilliantly talented squad had not gone far enough.

This time around could be a lot different though. The players mentioned have all performed impressively in the past 12 months, Martínez has developed a style that seems to work and Belgium also have wonderful strength in depth across their entire squad.

This could well be the tournament where Belgium finally prove they have what it takes to impress the whole sporting world.

> "We will have to play game by game. We have a great team with top-quality players, but we need to be strong as a unit."
>
> — Axel Witsel

HOW THEY QUALIFIED

Belgium enjoyed a straightforward qualification process for the 2018 FIFA World Cup as they topped Group G with some ease.

In a group containing Greece, Bosnia and Herzegovina, Estonia, Cyprus and Gibraltar, Belgium played ten matches, winning nine and drawing the other.

Their unbeaten passage to Russia was helped by scoring an incredible 43 times across their ten matches and conceding on just six occasions as they earned 28 points, nine clear of second-placed Greece.

Although Belgium were always the heavy favourites to qualify from their group, the manner in which they did it – and the phenomenal amount of goals they scored – just goes to show how dangerous they can be on their day.

They may feel slightly undercooked as a team and perhaps feel untested after cruising through qualifying but there is no chance complacency will be a problem for Martínez's men.

Belgium
Panama
Tunisia
England

GROUP **G**

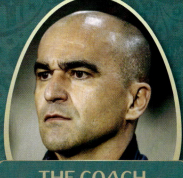

THE COACH

ALL-TIME TOP GOALSCORER
ROMELU LUKAKU
31

ALL-TIME MOST CAPS
JAN VERTONGHEN
98

HAT-TRICK OF HEROES

KEVIN DE BRUYNE

Kevin De Bruyne has been a revelation at Manchester City over the past two seasons and he is a wonderful footballer who is capable of unlocking any defence in the world on his day.

As well as having a keen eye for goal, De Bruyne is a wonderful passer of the ball, he works hard for the wider cause and is forever looking to attack.

Manchester City's squad has talent galore but there is a reason De Bruyne is considered one of their finest players and he now has the opportunity to thrill the watching world.

ROBERTO MARTÍNEZ

Roberto Martínez was a surprise appointment as Belgium's manager in August 2016 after being approached to replace Marc Wilmots.

Previous to his current role, he had managed Wigan Athletic and Everton in the Premier League - winning the FA Cup with unfancied Wigan in 2013 no less - and believes in playing a fluent, open and expressive game.

Martínez teams love to attack but he has also worked hard at making Belgium stronger in defence.

National hero status awaits him if he guides Belgium all the way in Russia.

EDEN HAZARD

Eden Hazard's abilities at Chelsea are well known and he just loves scoring goals.

Hazard is happy to go looking for the ball with defenders at both domestic and international level having learned to fear the attacker's quick feet.

Hazard's talents have helped Chelsea to two Premier League titles, the UEFA Europa League and the League Cup.

Chelsea's fans – like Belgium – expect the very best from the players on the pitch at Stamford Bridge and Hazard has never let them down. Expect more magic from him in Russia.

> "We have players who've now played in big matches against the biggest countries. We've got an exciting challenge ahead of us and we're really raising expectations among our fans. Our job is not to let them down."

ROMELU LUKAKU

Romelu Lukaku leads the attack at Manchester United and it takes a special sort of footballer to be given that position.

After impressing superbly at Everton, where his goal record was incredible, Lukaku moved to Old Trafford in 2017 and has continued his rich scoring form.

He does the same for Belgium and should be way out ahead as his country's all-time top goalscorer by the time he retires.

Lukaku can out-think defenders as easily as he can out-muscle them, his left foot is a devastating weapon and he is also good in the air. He is a natural goalscorer and Belgium's go-to forward when they need a slice of inspiration.

FIFA World Cup™ Record

1930 GS	1958 DNQ	1978 DNQ	1998 GS
1934 GS	1962 DNQ	1982 16	2002 16
1938 GS	1966 DNQ	1986 4th	2006 DNQ
1950 W	1970 GS	1990 16	2010 DNQ
1954 GS	1974 DNQ	1994 16	2014 QF

DNE = Did not enter, **DNQ** = Did not qualify, **W** = Withdrew, **R1** = Round 1, **R2** = Round 2, **GS** = Group Stages, **16** = Last 16, **QF** = Quarter-finals, **4th** = Fourth place, **3rd** = Third place, **RU** = Runners-up, **C** = Champions

Statistics up until February 2018

OFFICIAL 2018 FIFA WORLD CUP™ TOURNAMENT MAGAZINE **121**

GROUP G
Belgium
Panama
Tunisia
England

PANAMA

In the decades to come, 10 October 2017 is likely to become as famous and revered in Panama as 4 July is in the USA.

That was the day Panama created wonderful footballing history and again showed how much FIFA World Cup™ qualification matters. Before 10 October 2017, Panama had tussled and toiled for years in their bid to make it to a FIFA World Cup and ten qualifying campaigns had ended in defeat and disappointment.

However, that has all changed. Indeed, so momentous was Panama's qualification that the country's president, Juan Carlos Varela, even declared a national holiday in the wake of his nation's success, giving Panama's football-obsessed public the chance to truly celebrate.

"The voice of the people has been heard… tomorrow will be a national holiday," he wrote on a social media site. "You deserve it."

Panama certainly deserved to crack open the champagne because their qualification truly was a stunning and unique moment in the country's history – sporting or otherwise.

Their previous footballing success amounted to finishing as runners-up at the 2013 CONCACAF Gold Cup.

There is no doubt Panama have a mountain to climb in Russia and they are in a formidably strong group that will test them to their limits. Yet FIFA World Cup tournaments are about celebrating all the teams involved and wishing them well.

And, no matter what happens in Russia, nothing will stop the party in Panama.

> "It's a really significant achievement and something we deserve. We've been striving for this for a good while now and it all worked out."
> — Román Torres

HOW THEY QUALIFIED

Football's capacity to stun and inspire was there for everybody to see when Panama finally managed to make it to a FIFA World Cup.

Panama started the final matchday of qualifying in a great position but they needed to beat Costa Rica at home and Trinidad and Tobago would also have to do them a favour and beat the USA.

Fortunately for Panama, that is exactly what happened.

After going behind against Costa Rica in Panama City, Gabriel Torres headed them level before Román Torres struck in the 87th minute, and with Trinidad and Tobago also overcoming the USA 2-1, Panama had done enough to earn the points required to finish in a CONCACAF qualifying position.

What made their achievement all the more remarkable was the fact that they had never ever previously been in a CONCACAF qualifying position before, not even for 24 hours.

Belgium
Panama
Tunisia
England

GROUP G

FIFA WORLD CUP RUSSIA 2018

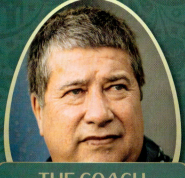

THE COACH

HERNÁN DARÍO GÓMEZ

Hernán Darío Gómez is a national hero in Panama after leading them to their first-ever FIFA World Cup tournament and the Colombian has done a simply wonderful job in steering the tiny nation to Russia.

After taking over in February 2014, Gómez brought plenty of experience to the Panama setup as he had previously helped Colombia to both the 1990 and 1994 FIFA World Cup™ editions as assistant coach before repeating the feat at the 1998 competition as the manager himself.

Four years later, he also took Ecuador to their first FIFA World Cup edition.

"Panama is currently at a point of learning, of progressing, it's a high level for Panama and we have to get a lot better but that's why we've come isn't it? To play against the big names."

ALL-TIME TOP GOALSCORER
LUIS TEJADA
43

ALL-TIME MOST CAPS
GABRIEL GÓMEZ
140

HAT-TRICK OF HEROES

JAIME PENEDO

Jaime Penedo has been Panama's first-choice goalkeeper for well over a decade and first played for his national side in June 2003.

He plays for Dinamo Bucharest in Romania's *Liga 1* and is regarded as a supremely confident and consistent performer and a player who brings plenty of solidity to Panama's defensive efforts.

Penedo is not the tallest goalkeeper but his athleticism, decision making and dead-ball skills are all first-class and he will be one of Panama's heroes if he can maintain a clean sheet in Russia.

ROMÁN TORRES

Román Torres was the hero of the hour for Panama when he scored the decisive goal that sealed FIFA World Cup qualification and he has been an integral member of Panama's side for a long time, having made his debut back in 2005.

Torres has captained Panama in the past and is looked upon with awe by many of the younger members of Panama's squad because of his consistency, commitment and desire to improve.

The defender plays domestically for Seattle Sounders FC in Major League Soccer and has made over 100 appearances for his country.

FIDEL ESCOBAR

Fidel Escobar plays for New York Red Bulls in Major League Soccer and the 23-year-old really is one of Panama's hottest prospects.

He made his national debut in 2015 after earlier shining for Panama's U-20 side. The central defender is extremely quick, strong in the tackle and in the air, and he reads the game very well for such a young player.

Escobar is undoubtedly going to become one of Panama's most important and respected players in the years to come and the 2018 FIFA World Cup™ is the perfect opportunity for him to showcase his talents.

FIFA World Cup™ Record

1930	DNE	1958	DNE	1978	DNQ	1998	DNQ
1934	DNE	1962	DNE	1982	DNQ	2002	DNQ
1938	DNE	1966	DNE	1986	DNQ	2006	DNQ
1950	DNE	1970	DNE	1990	DNQ	2010	DNQ
1954	DNE	1974	DNE	1994	DNQ	2014	DNQ

DNE = Did not enter, **DNQ** = Did not qualify, **W** = Withdrew, **R1** = Round 1, **R2** = Round 2, **GS** = Group Stages, **16** = Last 16, **QF** = Quarter-finals, **4th** = Fourth place, **3rd** = Third place, **RU** = Runners-up, **C** = Champions

Statistics up until February 2018

OFFICIAL 2018 FIFA WORLD CUP™ TOURNAMENT MAGAZINE **123**

GROUP G
Belgium
Panama
Tunisia
England

TUNISIA

Tunisia go into FIFA World Cup 2018™ with one goal in mind: to make history.

The North Africans are no strangers to the biggest tournament in world football but they have never managed to accumulate enough points to progress beyond the group stage.

Could this be the tournament when that situation changes?

The Tunisians have made FIFA World Cup™ history before. In 1978, making their first appearance at a finals, they became the first African team to win a game, beating Mexico 3-1. That win unlocked the door for a second African team to qualify for following tournament.

Since then Tunisia have qualified for three further FIFA World Cups in successive competitions between 1998 and 2006. Unfortunately, nine games in those tournaments have yielded no further wins but their World Cup finals matches so far have included creditable draws with Belgium, Romania and West Germany.

Technically excellent, and with players good enough to ply their trade in some of Europe's top divisions, Tunisia will feel they have the ability to trouble the world's best teams.

They are a nation with a proud history and can look back on a CAF Africa Cup of Nations victory in 2004 as their crowning glory when they defeated Morocco on home turf. They have also finished as runners-up twice.

Now, having had a 12-year gap between FIFA World Cups, the *Eagles of Carthage* are ready to remind football fans everywhere what they are capable of.

> "I can't tell you how happy I am to see all this joy on Tunisian faces. It's been a long time since we last qualified."
>
> — Mohamed Amine Ben Amor

HOW THEY QUALIFIED

Tunisia's road to Russia began in November 2015 when they overcame Mauritania in a two-legged tie to qualify for the final group stage where they were joined by Congo DR, Libya and Guinea in Group A.

A tight group, in which only the top team qualified for the FIFA World Cup, saw Tunisia go unbeaten, yet only finish one point above Congo DR with a 2-1 home win over the Central African side in September 2017 proving crucial.

Tunisia went into their final home game with the already-eliminated Libya needing just a point to qualify. They got it thanks to a 0-0 draw, but not without enduring a nervy afternoon.

Key to the Tunisians' success was a solid back line which only conceded four goals in their six group games.

At the other end, Youssef Msakni's three goals were enough to make him his country's top goalscorer in qualifying – all those goals coming when he scored a hat-trick in a 4-1 win over Guinea.

Belgium
Panama
Tunisia
England

GROUP **G**

FIFA WORLD CUP RUSSIA 2018

THE COACH

NABIL MAÂLOUL

The paths of the Tunisian national team and their coach, Nabil Maâloul, seem to keep crossing.

As a talented player, Maâloul earned 74 caps for his country before he ventured into the world of coaching.

As well as leading clubs in Tunisia and Qatar during his 20-year coaching career, he has been assistant coach of the national side and twice been the manager himself.

His latest stint began in 2017. Despite Tunisia leading World Cup qualifying Group A, a disappointing showing in the Africa Cup of Nations saw Henryk Kasperczak lose his job, allowing Maâloul the chance to lead his nation to Russia.

"My congratulations to the people of Tunisia for this successful qualification campaign. I knew the match against Libya would be tough and that the pressure would be on us. Tunisia showed what they are capable of."

ALL-TIME TOP GOALSCORER
ISSAM JEMÂA
36

ALL-TIME MOST CAPS
SADOK SASSI
116

HAT-TRICK OF HEROES

AYMEN MATHLOUTHI

Goalkeeper Aymen Mathlouthi is Tunisian through and through. One of the country's most experienced players, he has spent over a decade between the posts for the *Eagles of Carthage*.

Such is his ability, he has been monitored by clubs in Europe and elsewhere but he has always maintained his loyalty to his club, Étoile du Sahel.

The 33-year-old has been at his club since 2003 after spending two years with Club Africain.

He has won many honours with his club and helped Tunisia win the 2011 African Nations Championship.

WAHBI KHAZRI

Regular watchers of the Premier League will have spotted Wahbi Khazri's talent when he was plying his trade as an attacking midfielder for Sunderland.

Keen followers of Khazri's career would have seen his potential much earlier. Born in France, that is where he has otherwise spent most of his career, first with Bastia, then with Bordeaux, and recently on loan with Rennes.

Capable of scoring spectacular goals and dangerous when running with the ball, he made his international debut in 2013, having briefly appeared with France's U-21s.

YOUSSEF MSAKNI

If those unfamiliar with the Tunisian national team keep an eye on only one player from their squad at the 2018 FIFA World Cup™, Youssef Msakni should be that man.

An exciting talent with a real eye for goals, Msakni has attracted interest from big European clubs and his progress will be closely watched in Russia.

His hat-trick against Guinea during the FIFA World Cup™ qualifying campaign really caught the eye and he averages around a goal every other game for his club, Al Duhail, in the Qatar Stars League.

FIFA World Cup™ Record

1930	DNE	1958	DNE	1978	GS	1998	GS
1934	DNE	1962	DNQ	1982	DNQ	2002	GS
1938	DNE	1966	W	1986	DNQ	2006	GS
1950	DNE	1970	DNQ	1990	DNQ	2010	DNQ
1954	DNE	1974	DNQ	1994	DNQ	2014	DNQ

DNE = Did not enter, **DNQ** = Did not qualify, **W** = Withdrew, **R1** = Round 1, **R2** = Round 2, **GS** = Group Stages, **16** = Last 16, **QF** = Quarter-finals, **4th** = Fourth place, **3rd** = Third place, **RU** = Runners-up, **C** = Champions

Statistics up until February 2018

GROUP G
Belgium
Panama
Tunisia
England

ENGLAND

England, a nation for so long starved of World Cup glory, are looking forward to the 2018 FIFA World Cup Russia™ on the back of a positive qualification campaign and the form of some of their younger stars.

It is now 52 years since Bobby Moore lifted the Jules Rimet Trophy on home soil at Wembley as England rejoiced at their victory over West Germany but the time since has been barren for the side now managed by Gareth Southgate.

Southgate, who replaced Sam Allardyce as England manager in 2016, has a wonderfully attacking and vibrant squad at his disposal and he oversaw a consistent qualifying campaign.

For England's long-suffering supporters, they will take some comfort in the seemingly endless amount of raw talent coming through the youth system they have in place, and brilliant recent victories in the FIFA U-20 World Cup 2017 and FIFA U-17 World Cup 2017 have set the example for the senior side.

One of England's problems in the past has been a lack of cohesion and team spirit with huge stars not gelling together well enough on the pitch. However, Southgate has worked hard to foster a new England identity and team spirit.

England will, as usual, take a huge contingent of supporters to Russia to cheer Southgate's side on and the *Three Lions* players would dearly love to give their fans something to shout about at long last.

> "We want to win something for our country. That's the focus. What's done is done. Be that the way we performed at the last World Cup, or the way that Germany performed in Brazil. It's done now. Everything's up for grabs."
>
> — Joe Hart

HOW THEY QUALIFIED

England's qualification for the 2018 FIFA World Cup Russia contained few, if any, real glitches.

With eight wins from their ten qualification matches in Group F, England confirmed their attendance in Russia with a 1-0 victory over Slovenia at Wembley in October 2017.

In earlier contests, the late and dramatic point earned against Scotland at Hampden Park in June 2017 stands out as the most interesting performance as Harry Kane scored in the 93rd minute to protect England's unbeaten status.

The *Three Lions* will now be hoping to carry that unbeaten form with them into the tournament itself.

England have managed to qualify for major tournaments with ease in recent times but then failed to produce their best in the main event.

Their impressive qualifying performances should hopefully mean that life is different this time around in Russia.

Belgium
Panama
Tunisia
England

GROUP G

FIFA WORLD CUP RUSSIA 2018

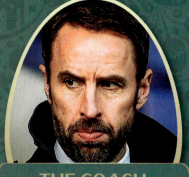

THE COACH

ALL-TIME TOP GOALSCORER
WAYNE ROONEY
53

ALL-TIME MOST CAPS
PETER SHILTON
125

HAT-TRICK OF HEROES

HARRY KANE

Harry Kane plays for Tottenham Hotspur and is undoubtedly one of the most potent strikers on the planet at the moment.

Consistently brilliant with both feet and also superb in the air, the unassuming Kane is the man England are looking to for goals at the 2018 FIFA World Cup Russia.

When Kane established himself at Tottenham in the 2014-15 season, he was not given the credit he deserved for his goalscoring and hard work.

However, Kane has more than proved his critics wrong and it looks as if nothing will stop him from becoming one of England's greatest-ever strikers.

GARETH SOUTHGATE

Gareth Southgate's most defining moment in an England shirt came when he missed a crucial penalty against Germany in the semi-final of UEFA EURO 1996. However, that will all be forgiven if he can lead England to FIFA World Cup glory in Russia.

Southgate is seen as a quiet, thoughtful individual who is keen to continue bringing through the next breed of England international.

He played 57 times for England as a central defender so knows exactly what it takes to thrive at the highest level.

England's players clearly respect his demeanour and working methods and Southgate is held in high regard in his home country.

DELE ALLI

Dele Alli plays alongside Harry Kane at Tottenham Hotspur and he is right up alongside Kane as a wonderfully gifted and thrilling footballer.

When Alli gets the ball, opposition defenders start to panic, such is his pace and ability, and he also likes to hit the back of the net himself.

Alli is all about attacking and making opportunities for himself and others. If he remains as sharp and as fit for England as he has been for Tottenham in recent times, the 2018 FIFA World Cup Russia could be a landmark tournament for the young man.

"To have played in a World Cup for my country was an incredible honour. To lead them there as a manager is beyond that."

KYLE WALKER

Kyle Walker is a man in his footballing prime.

The Manchester City right back has been given the opportunity by both Southgate and club manager Pep Guardiola to express himself and he has grabbed the chance with both hands.

Walker loves to attack as much as he loves to defend and he has the passing skills and talent to help unlock opposition defences when he does get forward.

He has spoken publicly many times about his excitement at representing England at the 2018 FIFA World Cup and he could be one of his country's most prominent performers.

FIFA World Cup™ Record

1930	DNE	1958	GS	1978	DNQ	1998	16
1934	DNE	1962	QF	1982	16	2002	QF
1938	DNE	1966	C	1986	QF	2006	QF
1950	GS	1970	QF	1990	4th	2010	16
1954	QF	1974	16	1994	DNQ	2014	GS

DNE = Did not enter, **DNQ** = Did not qualify, **W** = Withdrew, **R1** = Round 1, **R2** = Round 2, **GS** = Group Stages, **16** = Last 16, **QF** = Quarter-finals, **4th** = Fourth place, **3rd** = Third place, **RU** = Runners-up, **C** = Champions

Statistics up until February 2018

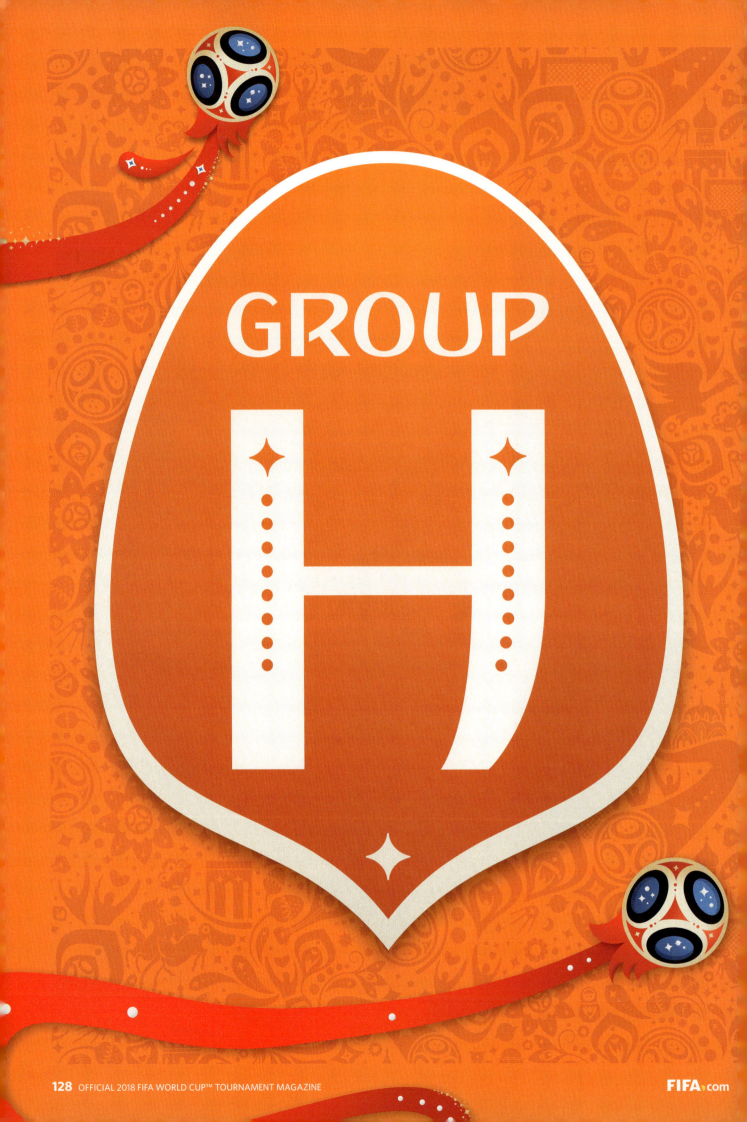

POLAND

SENEGAL

COLOMBIA

JAPAN

FIFA WORLD CUP RUSSIA 2018

Group H Fixtures

19 JUNE
Colombia v. Japan
13:00
Mordovia Arena, Saransk

19 JUNE
Poland v. Senegal
16:00
Spartak Stadium, Moscow

24 JUNE
Japan v. Senegal
16:00
Ekaterinburg Arena, Ekaterinburg

24 JUNE
Poland v. Colombia
19:00
Kazan Arena, Kazan

28 JUNE
Japan v. Poland
15:00
Volgograd Arena, Volgograd

28 JUNE
Senegal v. Colombia
15:00
Samara Arena, Samara

Kick-offs are UK time (UTC/GMT)

GROUP H
Poland
Senegal
Colombia
Japan

POLAND

Football fans of a certain age can't think of the Poland national team without recalling the great sides of the 1970s and early 1980s.

Sparked by the arrival of coach Kazimierz Górski, Poland enjoyed a period of success they hadn't seen before and haven't seen since, with stars like Grzegorz Lato, Zbigniew Boniek and Andrzej Szarmach leading the way.

The first sign of the excitement to come came when Poland won the gold medal at the 1972 Munich Olympics.

Their success then at the 1974 FIFA World Cup™ – also in Germany – shouldn't have been a shock, but it still caught a lot of people by surprise. They finished top of a group containing Italy and Argentina, then came runners-up in the second group stage, meaning they went into the third-place play-off, which they won against Brazil, with a goal from Lato, who finished as the tournament's top scorer.

Two years later they claimed another Olympic medal, this time a silver one, before a creditable FIFA World Cup™ performance in 1978 which saw them top a group containing West Germany before coming unstuck in the second group phase.

If anybody thought the Polish star was in decline, they were wrong. At the 1982 FIFA World Cup™ in Spain, they again managed to finish in third. In the semi-finals they lost out to Italy but beat France to finish third.

Recent FIFA World Cup performances haven't been as impressive, so having missed out on the last two tournaments, the Poles will be keen to make up for lost time.

> "My brother James Rodríguez... I remember your great goals during the last World Cup. I hope you will remember mine from Russia."
> — Robert Lewandowski

HOW THEY QUALIFIED

An outstanding qualifying performance saw Poland top a tough group, suffering only one defeat along the way.

In a group with Denmark, Romania, Montenegro, Armenia and Kazakhstan, the Poles managed to win eight of their matches, qualifying for Russia with a game to spare.

The fact they made it so comfortably was largely down to the prolific goal-getting of striker Robert Lewandowski.

The Bayern Munich front-man scored an amazing 16 goals in ten games to finish as Europe's top marksman in qualifiers and he managed to score three hat-tricks along the way.

Poland only suffered two hiccups in their ten matches. They could only manage a 2-2 draw in their opening game in Kazakhstan, while a 4-0 defeat in Denmark could have derailed a less confident group of players.

Poland won their final three games though and they will be a force to be reckoned with at the FIFA World Cup in Group H.

Poland
Senegal
Colombia
Japan

GROUP H

THE COACH

ADAM NAWAŁKA

Poland are on the rise again and the man leading the way is head coach Adam Nawałka.

Nawałka was a talented player himself in the 1970s and 1980s, playing most of his football with Wisła Kraków. He also made 34 appearances for the national team at a time when Poland was awash with top-quality footballers.

His managerial career has seen him take charge of several clubs – all in Poland – before he was handed the reins of the national team in 2013 following the departure of Waldemar Fornalik.

Nawałka has since led Poland to UEFA EURO 2016, and now he is preparing his team for the 2018 FIFA World Cup™.

"In the qualifiers we effectively scored 28 goals, so on average 2.8 per game. That's a good result. But we conceded 14, so 1.4 per game. That's too much. We know this and we will try to fix it."

ALL-TIME TOP GOALSCORER
ROBERT LEWANDOWSKI
51

ALL-TIME MOST CAPS
MICHAŁ ŻEWŁAKOW
102

HAT-TRICK OF HEROES

JAKUB BŁASZCZYKOWSKI

A genuine world-class talent and top-quality midfielder, Poland are lucky to have a player like Jakub Błaszczykowski to call upon.

He has been a regular in the national team for over a decade and has played for some huge clubs in Europe including Borussia Dortmund, Fiorentina and VfL Wolfsburg.

While at Dortmund he won the *Bundesliga* twice, played in a UEFA Champions League final and was twice named Polish Player of the Year.

A tricky player with an eye for a spectacular goal, he is closing in on the all-time appearances record for the national team, currently held by Michał Żewłakow with 102.

KAMIL GLIK

Kamil Glik has really blossomed as his career has evolved and at the age of 30 he is a key man for both Poland and his club, Monaco.

His nomadic early years as a footballer took him to Spain, Poland and Italy, but when he signed for Torino in 2011 things really took off for him.

When he eventually left the Italian club in 2016 to sign for Monaco, the dominant centre back went with his former club's blessing and he has gone on to win *Ligue 1* in France.

He has now made over 50 appearances for Poland and is crucial to their progress at the 2018 FIFA World Cup.

ROBERT LEWANDOWSKI

As goal machines go, few are as prolific as the incredible Robert Lewandowski.

Put simply: if Poland are to do well at the 2018 FIFA World Cup, they need their main man to keep scoring goals.

His importance is best illustrated by Poland's FIFA World Cup qualifying campaign. He scored in nine of their ten games. The only game he didn't score in was the only game the Poles lost.

Indeed, a hat-trick in one of those qualifiers, against Armenia, made him Poland's all-time top goalscorer.

Aged just 29 and still at the peak of his powers, he could extend that record to a figure that will go unchallenged for decades to come.

FIFA World Cup™ Record

1930	DNE	1958	DNQ	1978	R2	1998	DNQ
1934	DNE	1962	DNQ	1982	3rd	2002	GS
1938	R1	1966	DNQ	1986	16	2006	GS
1950	DNE	1970	DNQ	1990	DNQ	2010	DNQ
1954	DNE	1974	3rd	1994	DNQ	2014	DNQ

DNE = Did not enter, **DNQ** = Did not qualify, **W** = Withdrew, **R1** = Round 1, **R2** = Round 2, **GS** = Group Stages, **16** = Last 16, **QF** = Quarter-finals, **4th** = Fourth place, **3rd** = Third place, **RU** = Runners-up, **C** = Champions

Statistics up until February 2018

GROUP H
Poland
Senegal
Colombia
Japan

SENEGAL

It's been a long time coming but Senegal are once again contenders in a FIFA World Cup™.

It only feels like yesterday that they were electrifying the 2002 FIFA World Cup™ with some incredible performances, none more so than the tournament's wonderful opening-match victory over holders France.

That squad had some remarkable talents such as El-Hadji Diouf, Henri Camara, Papa Bouba Diop and Tony Sylva, who is now the national goalkeeper coach, but the time since those 2002 exploits has not been easy for the *Lions of Teranga*.

Their qualification for 2018 FIFA World Cup Russia™ should change all that and is a testament to some of the superb players they now have at their disposal.

Stars such as Sadio Mané, Diafra Sakho, Cheikhou Kouyaté, Keita Baldé and Idrissa Gueye are more than capable of providing Senegal with the quality and class they will need if they are to replicate 2002, when they got to the round of 16 in captivating manner.

The catalyst for Senegal's return to the world stage was their disappointing CAF Africa Cup of Nations 2015 showing under former coach Alain Giresse. A 2-0 group stage loss to Algeria saw Senegal go home early and they have not looked back from that moment on.

> "We've been successful due to our togetherness and solidarity, our desire to write our names in Senegalese football history in capital letters, and the 2002 generation, who have given our country a lot."
>
> — Saliou Ciss

HOW THEY QUALIFIED

A 2-0 victory over South Africa in Polokwane in November 2017 was enough for Senegal to claim qualification for the 2018 FIFA World Cup Russia and give Senegalese football fans a chance to see their heroes take on the world's best again.

A goal from Diafra Sakho gave Senegal an early lead in this crucial match before Thamsanqa Mkhize's late own goal ensured the *Lions of Teranga* had an unassailable lead at the top of Africa Group D.

Senegal began qualifying with a 2-0 win over Cape Verde Islands before consecutive draws against Burkina Faso.

However, another win over Cape Verde Islands in October 2017 meant that a win against South Africa would book their spot, and so it proved.

A further 2-1 victory over South Africa in their last qualifying match was academic in terms of qualification but it did allow them to top Africa Group D on 14 points, five clear of second-place Burkina Faso.

Poland | Senegal | Colombia | Japan

GROUP H

ALL-TIME TOP GOALSCORER
HENRI CAMARA
29

ALL-TIME MOST CAPS
HENRI CAMARA
99

THE COACH

ALIOU CISSÉ

Senegal will look to one of the heroes of their only previous FIFA World Cup showing, Aliou Cissé, for guidance in Russia.

Cissé was given the Senegal position immediately after the country was eliminated from the Africa Cup of Nations 2015 and he has gone from strength to strength in the period since. He is fondly remembered as the captain of the Senegal side from 2002 and his reputation in his home country remains good.

The former Paris St-Germain, Portsmouth and Lille midfielder played 35 times for his country between 1999 and 2005 and is now keen to turn the national side into an African footballing force.

"This is a great generation. What we're changing is the mindset. It's not just about playing a pass or some technical skill; it's about raising the whole level of African football. That's our objective."

HAT-TRICK OF HEROES

SADIO MANÉ

Sadio Mané is fast becoming an Anfield hero at Premier League giants Liverpool and he will be hoping to showcase his unbelievable talent to the whole world at the 2018 FIFA World Cup.

Blessed with superb pace and vision, Mané could set this tournament alight. He has struggled with injuries in the last two seasons, which have limited his playing time, but both Aliou Cissé and his domestic coach Jürgen Klopp have publicly acclaimed him as one of the best players in the world when he is fit and healthy.

Mané has a brilliant eye for goal and brings plenty of passion onto the pitch with him.

CHEIKHOU KOUYATÉ

Cheikhou Kouyaté is a central midfielder who plays in the Premier League for West Ham United. He has become a firm fans' favourite at the London side for his willingness to work box to box and Senegal will be hoping he is at his best during the FIFA World Cup.

Kouyaté is a tall, strong player who signed for West Ham in 2014 and he has been a standout performer for them and will be desperate to take his club form to Russia with him.

Manager Aliou Cissé clearly has faith in his abilities and has earmarked Kouyaté as one of his key performers at the 2018 FIFA World Cup Russia.

IDRISSA GUEYE

Idrissa Gueye plays for Everton in the Premier League and has become an increasingly important lynchpin for Senegal.

His tough-tackling displays and endless stamina mean he is a superb asset to any team and he will run all day for club and country.

He took a little while to settle into English football but he has matured into a real leader for Everton and nobody works harder for his team's cause than the defensive midfielder.

The 28-year-old learned his trade at Lille where he played over 100 matches before leaving for Aston Villa. He signed for his current club in 2016.

FIFA World Cup™ Record

1930	DNE	1958	DNE	1978	DNQ	1998	DNQ
1934	DNE	1962	DNE	1982	DNQ	2002	QF
1938	DNE	1966	W	1986	DNQ	2006	DNQ
1950	DNE	1970	DNQ	1990	DNQ	2010	DNQ
1954	DNE	1974	DNQ	1994	DNQ	2014	DNQ

DNE = Did not enter, **DNQ** = Did not qualify, **W** = Withdrew, **R1** = Round 1, **R2** = Round 2, **GS** = Group Stages, **16** = Last 16, **QF** = Quarter-finals, **4th** = Fourth place, **3rd** = Third place, **RU** = Runners-up, **C** = Champions

Statistics up until February 2018

GROUP H
Poland
Senegal
Colombia
Japan

COLOMBIA

Colombians are hoping they are going to enjoy a new golden age of football for their country.

For the first time since the 1990s, Colombia have reached consecutive FIFA World Cup™ tournaments and with an experienced coach in José Pékerman in charge of an extremely talented squad of players, hopes are high they can make their mark.

Last time out, at the 2014 FIFA World Cup™ in Brazil, Colombia achieved their best-ever result by reaching the quarter-finals, eventually losing out to the hosts 2-1. It was a success built on a mix of established world-class stars and a sprinkling of emerging young players who proved they have what it takes.

The brightest star in 2014 was James Rodríguez. Aged 22, he finished with the Golden Boot and also won the Goal of the Tournament.

He and his team-mates will be aiming to gain the same affection in their nation's hearts as the stars of the 1990s. Colombia qualified for the FIFA World Cup in 1990, 1994 and 1998 with legends like Carlos Valderrama, Faustino Asprilla and Freddy Rincón making huge contributions.

They entered the 1994 edition as one of the tournament favourites on the back of outstanding results like the 5-0 qualifying victory away at Argentina, but couldn't live up to expectations as they were knocked out at the group stage.

It was in 2001 that Colombia had their greatest international success, though, winning the *Copa América* for the only time in their history when it was held on home soil.

> "I missed the World Cup in Brazil and then had two horrible years. But now I'm going to Russia. God gave me confidence and I know I can keep on succeeding."
> — Ramadel Falcao

HOW THEY QUALIFIED

Colombia claimed the fourth and final automatic qualifying spot from the South American group, edging ahead of Peru who had to go into a play-off.

A rollercoaster qualifying campaign looked to be going well with four games to go after a 2-0 win against Ecuador in Quito put them in a commanding position.

As it turned out, a win in one of those final four games would have been enough to earn a ticket to Russia, but that was when the wins dried up. A 0-0 stalemate in Venezuela was followed by a creditable 1-1 draw with Brazil, Radamel Falcao grabbing an equaliser after Willian had opened the scoring.

The real problem came when Paraguay scored two late goals to condemn Colombia to a 2-1 defeat in their penultimate match.

Their fate remained in their own hands though. A win against Peru in the final match would earn certain qualification. As it turned out, results elsewhere meant a 1-1 draw was enough.

Poland
Senegal
Colombia
Japan

GROUP **H**

FIFA WORLD CUP RUSSIA 2018

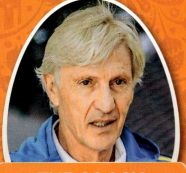

THE COACH

ALL-TIME TOP GOALSCORER
RAMADEL FALCAO
28

ALL-TIME MOST CAPS
CARLOS VALDERRAMA
111

HAT-TRICK OF HEROES

JOSÉ PÉKERMAN

José Pékerman is so well loved in his adopted homeland that he was handed Colombian citizenship by President Juan Manuel Santos, despite having been born in Argentina.

That kind of popularity has come about because of the reputation he has built, having helped Colombia to qualify for two successive FIFA World Cups after going 16 years without qualifying.

Pékerman gained recognition initially as a youth team coach in Argentina and Chile before leading the Argentina Under-20s to three FIFA World Youth Championships.

He then took the senior Argentina side to the quarter-finals of the 2006 FIFA World Cup™.

He has coached Colombia since 2012 and he now wants to take them to the next level.

> "I wanted a balanced group and I think we've got that. When you get to a World Cup the past is not important, every team starts from scratch... The most exciting thing is Colombia are here."

RAMADEL FALCAO

Colombia's top goalscorer of all time is a natural finisher who has scored goals everywhere he's been.

His first big club was River Plate in Argentina, before he moved to Europe with Porto and then Atlético Madrid.

A big-money move to Monaco followed and the goals kept flowing but a cruciate knee ligament injury set him back in 2013.

After loan spells with Manchester United and Chelsea, he's spent the 2017-18 season back at Monaco.

Among other honours, he became the first player to win the UEFA Europa League with two different clubs in consecutive seasons with Porto and Atlético Madrid in 2011 and 2012.

JAMES RODRÍGUEZ

One of the most recognisable faces at the 2018 FIFA World Cup™, James Rodríguez goes to Russia aiming to do the almost-impossible...improve on what he did four years ago.

In 2014 he scored the goal of the tournament in Brazil, a screaming volley against Uruguay, and finished as the top goalscorer in the competition.

His potential has always been there. He scored his first senior goal, for his club Banfield in Argentina, when aged just 17. At 20 he made his debut for the Colombia senior team.

Rodríguez already has 20 goals for his country so Radamel Falcao's national goals record might not be his for long.

JUAN CUADRADO

A direct, pacy, skilful wing man, Juan Cuadrado is the sort of player who gives opposing full-backs nightmares.

He started out at Independiente Medellín in Colombia but has spent most of his career in Italy, first with Udinese, but taking in spells at Lecce and Fiorentina. A brief stint with Chelsea, where he won the Premier League title, was preceded by a move to Juventus, where he has been starring again this season.

He scored on his Colombia debut in 2010 and has enjoyed a successful international career, which saw him finish as joint-top assist-maker at the 2014 FIFA World Cup, along with Germany's Toni Kroos.

FIFA World Cup™ Record

Year	Result	Year	Result	Year	Result	Year	Result
1930	DNE	1958	DNQ	1978	DNQ	1998	GS
1934	DNE	1962	GS	1982	DNQ	2002	DNQ
1938	W	1966	DNQ	1986	DNQ	2006	DNQ
1950	DNE	1970	DNQ	1990	16	2010	DNQ
1954	DNE	1974	DNQ	1994	GS	2014	QF

DNE = Did not enter, **DNQ** = Did not qualify, **W** = Withdrew, **R1** = Round 1, **R2** = Round 2, **GS** = Group Stages, **16** = Last 16, **QF** = Quarter-finals, **4th** = Fourth place, **3rd** = Third place, **RU** = Runners-up, **C** = Champions

Statistics up until February 2018

GROUP H
Poland
Senegal
Colombia
Japan

JAPAN

A year before the Rugby World Cup, which will be held in Japan for the first time in 2019, it is the 2018 FIFA World Cup™ that is occupying Japanese hearts and minds at the moment.

Having now qualified for the past six FIFA World Cups™, Japan are a nation that have not looked back since first qualifying for the tournament in 1998.

The opening 15 tournaments did not contain the *Samurai Blue* but round-of-16 finishes on home soil in 2002 and in South Africa in 2010 have helped Japan blossom into a side that believes it can compete at the highest level.

Four years ago, Japan were the first nation to qualify for the 2014 FIFA World Cup™ in Brazil but they never really got going and will be desperately determined to do better this time around.

If they are to succeed in Russia, they will expect some magic from the likes of Shinji Kagawa, Yuya Osako and Keisuke Honda.

Japan tend to play a high-paced and high-tempo game, looking to use their athleticism and fitness levels to grind opposition sides down.

They are not short of goalscorers either and they tend to spread the scoring around rather than rely on one individual to hit the back of the net.

Japan's FIFA World Cup history has been hit and miss with round-of-16 success in some tournaments mixed in with drab group-stage exits in others. Their aim in Russia is to get back to winning ways and do their best to still be in the mix when the knockout stages begin.

> "I think we should keep writing history with even better results. This is our role, and we have to carry this on to the next generation."
> — Genki Haraguchi

HOW THEY QUALIFIED

Japan were pushed right to the very edge in their attempts to qualify for Russia and just about did enough to pip Saudi Arabia and Australia to the top spot in Asian Football Confederation's Group B.

They booked their place at the 2018 FIFA World Cup Russia with a winner-takes-all fixture with Australia at Saitama Stadium in August last year. Both sides knew that a victory would be enough to secure their qualification and it was Japan who came out on top thanks to goals from Takuma Asano and Yosuke Ideguchi.

In earlier contests, Japan had mixed fortunes, losing to United Arab Emirates early on but they then kicked into top gear, winning six of their ten matches, scoring 17 times and conceding on seven occasions.

Japan have a lovely balance between goalscoring effectiveness and defensive efficiency and that served them well in qualifying and will have to do the same in Russia.

Poland
Senegal
Colombia
Japan

GROUP H

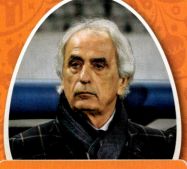

THE COACH

VAHID HALILHODŽIĆ

Vahid Halilhodžić has a mixed FIFA World Cup history involving both great joy and great disappointment.

He helped Côte d'Ivoire qualify for the 2010 FIFA World Cup South Africa™ but was sacked before the tournament began.

Then he did wonderfully well to steer Algeria to the round of 16 four years later in 2014. Halilhodžić is a strict disciplinarian and has spoken of his delight in working with a Japan team that obeys him to the letter.

If Japan are to prosper in Russia, their players will have to once again adhere to their manager's style of play and hard-to-beat mentality.

"The Japanese are respectful, serious people who like to see a job well done. That attitude has really helped me with my work and with implementing my coaching methods."

ALL-TIME TOP GOALSCORER
KUNISHIGE KAMAMOTO
80

ALL-TIME MOST CAPS
YASUHITO ENDŌ
152

HAT-TRICK OF HEROES

SHINJI OKAZAKI

Shinji Okazaki was the talk of his homeland in 2016 when he was part of Leicester City's truly remarkable Premier League-winning season.

Although Jamie Vardy and Riyad Mahrez picked up most of the plaudits for Leicester's success, Okazaki was also a massive part of their triumph.

He is a pacy striker who has more than settled into English football despite not being the tallest or most physical of players.

With a half-century of goals already for Japan, he is well on his way to national hero status and can cement his reputation even further in Russia.

SHINJI KAGAWA

Shinji Kagawa is another Japan player who is a full-blown national hero at home.

The Borussia Dortmund star has played in the *Bundesliga* since 2010 and although he took a while to settle, the Dortmund fans have full respect for an attacking midfielder capable of tearing teams apart.

Kagawa's greatest strength is his determination to go looking for the ball and to get into attacking positions as often as possible. He is a generous team-mate and is always looking to play the killer ball to help his side get into goalscoring positions.

YUYA KUBO

Yuya Kubo could be a world sensation by the time the 2018 FIFA World Cup Russia is concluded.

Aged just 24, the Gent striker appears to have a complete game and is at the start of what could be a very successful career both domestically and internationally.

He is a hard-working forward who likes to go looking for the ball and having played for every Japan youth side from U-16 onwards, he is immersed in Japan's footballing style and culture.

He could truly be one of the breakout performers in Russia and he is desperate to get started and showcase his skills.

FIFA World Cup™ Record

1930	DNE	1958	DNE	1978	DNQ	1998	GS
1934	DNE	1962	DNQ	1982	DNQ	2002	16
1938	W	1966	DNE	1986	DNQ	2006	GS
1950	DNE	1970	DNQ	1990	DNQ	2010	16
1954	DNQ	1974	DNQ	1994	DNQ	2014	GS

DNE = Did not enter, **DNQ** = Did not qualify, **W** = Withdrew, **R1** = Round 1, **R2** = Round 2, **GS** = Group Stages, **16** = Last 16, **QF** = Quarter-finals, **4th** = Fourth place, **3rd** = Third place, **RU** = Runners-up, **C** = Champions

Statistics up until February 2018

TEARS OF JOY

FIFA WORLD CUP™ LEGEND AND FIFA FAN FEST™ AMBASSADOR MARCEL DESAILLY LOOKS TO THE PAST, PRESENT AND FUTURE TO HIGHLIGHT JUST HOW MUCH THIS TOURNAMENT MEANS TO PEOPLE

"Even now, people stop me in the street and they are almost crying as they try and thank me."

That quote alone encapsulates exactly what winning a FIFA World Cup means to fans around the world and also why, 20 years on, Marcel Desailly remains as big a footballing legend today as he was two decades ago.

Desailly, of course, was a member of Aimé Jacquet's side that stunned the sporting world – and brought Paris and France to an ecstatic standstill – one July 1998 evening at the Stade de France when France overcame heavy favourites Brazil to lift the Official Trophy.

The former AC Milan and Chelsea great was one of the finest defenders in the history of the game and looks back with great fondness on France's win.

But as well as looking backwards, Desailly, who is now a FIFA Fan Fest ambassador, is just as keen to look forwards and celebrate what will be a thrilling 2018 FIFA World Cup™ in Russia.

"12 July will be the 20th anniversary of our win and it has gone fast!" he said.

"When you talk about football memories, winning the World Cup changed my life a lot. When I look back, the memories and emotions sometimes seem stronger now than they did then.

"It allowed me to be a different man in the eyes of the French people. It was a tough tournament for us and I was used to playing at a high level with high commitment at AC Milan but that was nothing compared to what the atmosphere and pressure is like at a World Cup.

"Sometimes great club players don't perform at international level but we had players who were just as comfortable in a France shirt as a club shirt so we managed to digest the pressure and translate that into some good performances. We were not paralysed, we managed to deliver and you could not see how we would lose it at home."

Surprisingly, according to Desailly, France's glory in the final on home soil, when a Zinédine Zidane masterclass helped *Les Bleus* to victory, was not as difficult as other matches in the tournament.

He added: "My memories are not so much about the final actually. I remember the first match against South Africa and we were

EXCLUSIVE INTERVIEW

FIFA Fan Fest ambassadors Marcel Desailly and (left) Aleksandr Kerzhakov.

all shaking in the dressing room as the South African side sang a song in the tunnel. We were almost paralysed by the pressure. But we came through that well and, if anything, the final was the easiest match we played. It felt like there was no way, no way, we were going to allow it to slip now.

"We knew that it was for us. We were not the best team at the time – Argentina, Brazil and the Netherlands were better than us – but we knew that playing at home meant this final was for us. There didn't feel like too much pressure in the final. It went exactly as Aimé said it would. He had told us: 'They're not good on free kicks guys, we will get opportunities from them, let's concentrate, be patient and take our chances and everything will go correct.' He was right and it was a dream – a big, beautiful dream."

Just as France benefitted from home support two decades ago, so Desailly believes Russia can make a significant and enjoyable impact at the 2018 FIFA World Cup, and he is hopeful that they can keep their fans excited until the latter stages of the tournament.

And although he has pinpointed Brazil as a team to watch, he believes this tournament will be too close and too difficult to call.

"Playing at home gives you an extra boost and when you talk about football, you talk about the development of football and I really think Russia will perform well," he said. "I think, with

> "Playing at home gives you an extra boost and when you talk about football, you talk about the development of football and I really think Russia will perform well."

France's 1998 FIFA World Cup winners

EXCLUSIVE INTERVIEW

> "This World Cup is going to be such a big success. The Russian people are ready for the most beautiful and important competition."

Kylian Mbappé is part of a strong French squad

Desailly with Fabien Barthez shortly after claiming the official trophy

their team spirit, their fans will really enjoy this tournament because we want the game of football to be so important in Russia.

"Brazil look fantastic at the moment and we also saw how good Germany were in the Confederations Cup so they will be even stronger at the World Cup. France, obviously, look like they have a lot of potential. We have a lot of new players in the national side and they've had to adapt to the higher level and the expectations of the national side but I am confident.

"Then there is Argentina and although they struggled to qualify, usually during the competition itself they perform."

As a FIFA Fan Fest ambassador, one issue that is close to Desailly's heart is his desire to see fans from all countries, wearing all colours, celebrating, enjoying and remembering a World Cup that should provide plenty of thrills and spills.

There are 11 FIFA Fan Fest sites dotted across Russia for the tournament and thousands of fans will be able to watch their heroes while being entertained in a safe atmosphere in a party environment.

"I'm so happy for the fans and for football," Desailly added. "This World Cup is going to be such a big success. The Russian people are ready for the most beautiful and important competition and the Russian government is so motivated to provide great stadiums and great infrastructure.

"The cities waiting to host games are just tremendous, with amazing cultures and histories, and visitors are going to have a wonderful time.

"On a tourist level it's going to be well organised and exciting. The Fan Fests mean supporters can get together in special areas that will be safe and where you can share in the atmosphere of the World Cup. You will be able to express your happiness – or your sadness! – and meet people from different cultures and countries.

"Sharing experiences and excitement with other people is so important and you can also support your team. The Fan Fests are there to promote beautiful family moments and that is what sport should be about."

OFFICIAL 2018 FIFA WORLD CUP™ TOURNA

2018 FIFA WORLD CUP™ IN NUMBERS

20
The number of teams that appeared at the 2014 FIFA World Cup™ in Brazil that will also be in Russia.

3
The number of hat-tricks scored by Robert Lewandowski in qualifying matches for this World Cup. He scored 16 goals in total.

36
The number of years since Peru last appeared at a FIFA World Cup™ – in Spain back in 1982.

16
Former Germany striker Miroslav Klose holds the record for the highest number of goals scored at FIFA World Cup tournaments with 16, scored between 2002-2014.

13
The highest number of goals scored at a single FIFA World Cup is 13, which France's Just Fontaine managed in 1958.

155,000
The estimated number of miles travelled by Australia as they came through 22 qualifying matches to reach the 2018 FIFA World Cup.

871

The total number of matches played in the Russia 2018 qualifiers, a record. The first took place in Timor-Leste on 12 March 2015 and the last in Peru on 15 November 2017.

171

The most goals scored in a finals tournament is 171, a number reached in both 1998 and 2014.

517

Italy's Walter Zenga holds the record for the goalkeeper to play the most consecutive minutes without conceding a goal in FIFA World Cup finals matches. He did it in 1990 and managed 517 minutes.

DEUTSCHER FUSSBALL-BUND

224

Germany have scored 224 goals in FIFA World Cup finals matches – more than any other team.

5

Russia's Oleg Salenko is the only man ever to have scored five goals in one FIFA World Cup finals match – in a 6-1 win against Cameroon in 1994.

17

The youngest player to score a hat-trick at a FIFA World Cup was Pelé, aged just 17 years and 244 days, at the 1958 FIFA World Cup™ in Sweden.

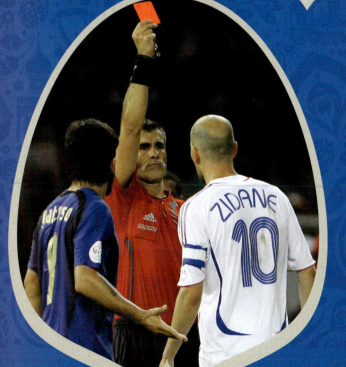

345

The 2006 FIFA World Cup™ in Germany kept referees very busy. Not only were there more yellow cards shown at the tournament (345) than any other, it also saw the most sendings-off (28).

EXCLUSIVE INTERVIEW

THE BIG STAGE

DANISH STAR CHRISTIAN ERIKSEN HOPING TO MAKE EXPERIENCE COUNT

Interview Jon Rayner

Christian Eriksen was just a teenager on the periphery of Denmark's team when they were last at a FIFA World Cup™...now he's the main man as they prepare to take to the world stage once again.

The midfield magician, who will be 26 by the time this summer's tournament in Russia comes around, had enjoyed a whirlwind year back in 2010 which culminated in him being the youngest player to participate at that summer's FIFA World Cup in South Africa.

He was only 17 when handed his senior first-team debut for Dutch giants Ajax in January 2010, turned 18 the following month, won his first Danish cap that March and was selected by then-manager Morten Olsen a few months later as part of Denmark's 23-man squad for the 2010 FIFA World Cup™.

By the time Eriksen stepped onto the pitch late in the second half of Denmark's opening Group E match against the Netherlands in Johannesburg, he had just 95 minutes of international football under his belt, but with a reputation as one of the most promising youngsters in Europe.

And here we are, some eight years later, Tottenham Hotspur's creative playmaker fulfilling his potential for club and country, scoring the goals which helped steer Denmark through their qualifying campaign and into the fifth FIFA World Cup in their history.

"It will certainly be very different for me this time around as I'm going to the tournament as an older and much more experienced player than I was back in South Africa," explained the highest scoring Danish footballer in Premier League history.

"Last time I was just a young guy who popped up on the international scene just before the tournament, got selected for the national team and I felt very lucky to be involved.

"I didn't feel any pressure though as I was on the outside of the team looking in, I was just trying to make my way in the game then and I was at the development stage of my career. I just tried to work hard in training and hopefully get some minutes on the pitch."

Fortunately for Christian, he managed to do exactly that, playing 17 minutes against the Netherlands and 27 minutes in their final

group match against Japan. Unfortunately though, Denmark lost both games and, despite beating Cameroon 2-1 in a game in which Eriksen didn't feature, they failed to make the knockout stages.

"Of course it was disappointing to head home early, but it was a great experience for a young player and a lot of fun.

"The one thing I did miss out on though was the qualifying matches. Most of the other guys in the squad had been battling for almost two years to reach the tournament, whereas I just turned up with the team at the World Cup.

"I've been through the qualification process since and I now know how good it feels to qualify and how bad it is to not make it. To qualify for the World Cup again this summer is a big thing for a small country like Denmark and we are all happy to be there once more."

And what a qualifying campaign it was for Eriksen.

The great Dane scored against all five nations in Group E, netting eight times as his country finished second in the group behind Poland to book a play-off berth in which they faced the Republic of Ireland over two legs.

Having been held to a goalless draw in Copenhagen in the first match, there was a certain amount of trepidation within the Danish camp when they travelled to Dublin for the return. But they needn't have worried as

> "It will always be a special moment in my career, but if things keep going as well as they are then who knows...there could be better moments ahead."

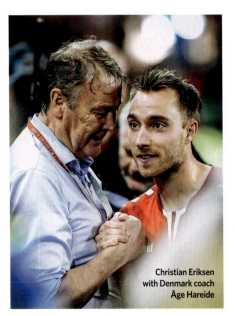

Christian Eriksen with Denmark coach Åge Hareide

Christian and his team-mates were fantastic on the night, producing an outstanding performance with Eriksen scoring a sublime hat-trick to over-turn Ireland's early goal, with Andreas Christensen and Nicklas Bendtner also on target in their 5-1 win.

"That was a very good night in Dublin," Christian said with a knowing smile. "It was 100 per cent one of the highlights of my career. Scoring a hat-trick to help your country qualify for the World Cup – it doesn't really get much better than that!

"In the home game, we couldn't create as much as we wanted, although we did still have chances, and we expected a tough game in the second match. We were 1-0 down after six minutes but it was a real lift to come back into it and lead 2-1 at half-time. To score three more in the second half was fantastic for us and our supporters.

"It will always be a special moment in my career, but if things keep going as well as they

EXCLUSIVE INTERVIEW

> "We did well in the 1986 FIFA World Cup in Mexico too, we showed what we are capable of and then went and won the Euros six years later. It's football and anything can happen."

are then who knows...there could be better moments ahead."

Danish supporters will obviously be hoping those moments happen soon and, while success on a global scale seems unlikely in Russia this summer, Christian will point to his own country's incredible triumph at UEFA EURO 1992 as a reason why the unexpected should never be ruled out.

Denmark failed to qualify for that tournament in nearby Sweden, finishing second in their qualifying group behind then-Yugoslavia. But troubles in the eastern European country led to the Yugoslavs being banned from competing, with Denmark called up to replace them just two weeks before the competition began. They then produced one of football's greatest-ever fairytales by going all the way to the final and beating Germany to lift the trophy against all the odds.

"I was literally just a few months old at the time but I've seen the movie that was made and plenty of video clips, it was obviously our country's biggest achievement," said Eriksen, currently with 21 goals in 75 appearances for Denmark.

"We did well in the 1986 FIFA World Cup in Mexico too, we showed what we are capable of and then went and won the Euros six years later. It's football and anything can happen.

"We have a difficult group alongside Peru, Australia and France, but our aim is to qualify from the group and see how far we can go from there. The tournament is a few months away still, but I know the supporters back home are excited and I'm sure they will travel in their numbers to Russia to come and cheer us on.

"It's a huge event and the whole country can't wait."

FIFA WORLD CUP™ TOURNAMENT MAGAZINE 147

TROPHY TOUR

The Official Trophy in Sri Lanka

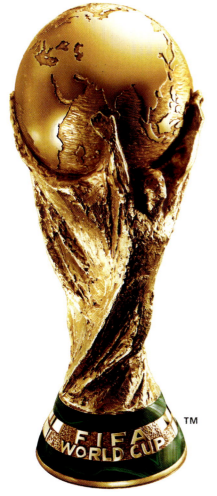

A MUCH TRAVELLED TROPHY

Bringing the excitement and joy of the FIFA World Cup™ to supporters all over the globe

Here is a quick question for football-mad friends and family: what is 36.5 centimetres tall, made from 11 pounds of gold, can only be held by a select few people and has already been around the globe three times this past year?

The answer, of course, is simple: the FIFA World Cup Trophy.

Every major sporting contest likes to believe that its silverware is the most iconic in the world but the FIFA World Cup Trophy is the only one that can claim to be truly recognisable in all four corners of the planet.

And it is to those four corners that the FIFA World Cup Trophy has been heading since September 2017 when it embarked on a monumental 149,576.78 kilometre trip that is the equivalent of travelling over three times around Earth, calling in at 90 different countries.

Sponsored by Coca-Cola, the trip of a lifetime is the longest journey the FIFA World Cup Trophy has ever been on, and over 800,000 people have had the chance to be photographed with the trophy.

Although each winning nation receives a replica of the trophy, the 'real' one lives in the FIFA World Football Museum in Zurich and only leaves Switzerland for the Final Draw for the FIFA World Cup™ and the final match of every World Cup.

FIFA.com

TROPHY TOUR

"The FIFA World Cup Trophy Tour by Coca-Cola is a rare opportunity for fans to see the Original Trophy up close"

Indeed, only previous winners of the World Cup and any heads of state are actually allowed to lift it because it is so precious and such a special trophy.

As the start of the 2018 FIFA World Cup™ gets closer and closer, the trophy will continue its journey across six continents before returning to Russia in May, just ahead of the tournament.

A FIFA spokesperson said: "In 2006, FIFA and long-term partner Coca-Cola took an ambitious first step on a remarkable new journey by taking the original FIFA World Cup Trophy and flying it around the world in the build-up to the 2006 FIFA World Cup in Germany. That first-ever FIFA World Cup Trophy Tour brought the energy and excitement of the world's most-loved football tournament, and its most coveted prize, directly to fans for the first time.

"Since 2006, every new edition of the FIFA World Cup has brought with it the promise of a new Trophy Tour travelling and touching down in new cities and meeting new fans. The FIFA World Cup Trophy Tour by Coca-Cola is a rare opportunity for fans to see the Original Trophy up close and have their experience captured with a photograph. It's an exciting and exclusive experience."

Have you missed your chance to see a piece of FIFA World Cup history? Head to www.fifa.com/worldcup/trophy-tour/ to see where on the planet the most famous trophy of all currently is.

FIFA World Cup winners Bebeto and David Trezeguet

The Official Trophy in Moscow

FIFA.com

That magical feeling

Arms in the air, an ecstatic expression on his face, ticker tape on the ground...this is one of the iconic FIFA World Cup™ images. It is from the 1978 final and shows Argentinian ace Mario Kempes running to celebrate, having just scored his second goal against the Netherlands to put the hosts 2-1 up in extra-time. Daniel Bertoni (right) later sealed a 3-1 win in Buenos Aires to give Argentina their first FIFA World Cup™ crown.

20 TOURNAMENTS: MAGIC MEMORIES

A whistle-stop tour of 88 years of football history

MAGIC MEMORIES

1930 URUGUAY
Teams involved: 13
Goals scored: 70
Golden Boot: Guillermo Stábile (ARG) 8
Winners: Uruguay

The first-ever FIFA World Cup™ was held in the Uruguayan city of Montevideo and home support was clearly crucial as Uruguay lifted the trophy at the Estadio Centenario.

Apart from the Yugoslavian squad, the European teams involved travelled to the tournament together, setting sail from Barcelona on the SS Conte Verde.

But it was two South American teams who would contest the final as Uruguay beat neighbours Argentina 4-2, with their final goal being scored by Hector Castro, a remarkable feat considering he only had one arm following a childhood accident. The FIFA World Cup had its first victors and international football would never be the same again.

1934 ITALY
Teams involved: 16
Goals scored: 70
Golden Boot: Oldřich Nejedlý (CZH) 5
Winners: Italy

Once again, home advantage proved to be the key to success as the Azzurri won the first of their four FIFA World Cup™ titles.

The World Cup had already begun to grow as eight Italian cities hosted matches as opposed to just Montevideo in the first edition four years previously.

After a thrilling final finished 1-1 after 90 minutes, Italy finally found the quality needed to break down opponents Czechoslovakia as Enrico Guaita crossed for Angelo Schiavio, and he scored to give Italy a 2-1 win and their first taste of FIFA World Cup glory.

1938 FRANCE
Teams involved: 15
Goals scored: 84
Golden Boot: Leônidas (BRA) 8
Winners: Italy

Italy became the first nation to retain the FIFA World Cup™ crown as they took the honours in Paris after a tournament in which Brazil, and Golden Boot winner Leônidas, had arguably shone the brightest.

France became the first host nation not to win the World Cup as they lost to Italy in the last eight before a brace each from Gino Colaussi and Silvio Piola helped the Italians to defeat an impressive Hungary side in the final, held at the Stade Olympique Colombes on 19 June 1938.

1950 BRAZIL
Teams involved: 13
Goals scored: 88
Golden Boot: Ademir (BRA) 8
Winners: Uruguay

As the world emerged from the shadows of World War Two, Uruguay were the victors as they won the FIFA World Cup™ for the second time, again on South American soil.

For the first time, the overall attendance for a World Cup passed the one million mark as 1,045,246 spectators watched the 22 matches.

The Maracanã witnessed a wonderful final – and a huge shock – as home favourites Brazil lost 2-1 thanks to goals from Juan Schiaffino and Alcides Ghiggia; a defeat for Brazil that is still one of the most significant in FIFA World Cup history.

1954 SWITZERLAND
Teams involved: 16
Goals scored: 140
Golden Boot: Sándor Kocsis (HUN) 11
Winners: West Germany

A goalscoring explosion saw the 1954 FIFA World Cup™ feature more goals than any other edition so far, and by a comfortable margin as well.

Hungary's Magical Magyars were the heavy favourites for the tournament and went into the final against West Germany unbeaten in 31 matches.

However, goals from Max Morlock and a brace from Helmut Rahn meant the Hungarians – including the legendary Ferenc Puskás – lost 3-2 and went home empty handed.

1958 SWEDEN
Teams involved: 16
Goals scored: 126
Golden Boot: Just Fontaine (FRA) 13
Winners: Brazil

The 1958 FIFA World Cup™ is best remembered for Brazil's first victory in the tournament and also the emergence of a young player by the name of Pelé.

The 17-year-old was playing in his first World Cup and he and his countrymen took it by storm.

Sweden were almost as impressive in their run to meet Brazil in the final. However, the Seleção came out on top in a 5-2 victory that saw Pelé – or Edson Arantes do Nascimento to give him his full name – score twice to break Sweden's hearts.

1962 CHILE
Teams involved: 16
Goals scored: 89
Golden Boot: Flórián Albert (HUN), Valentin Ivanov (Soviet Union), Dražan Jerković (YUG), Leonel Sánchez (CHI), Vavá (BRA), Garrincha (BRA) 4
Winners: Brazil

Brazil crossed the Andes and defended the FIFA World Cup™ crown they had won four years earlier in a tournament where they were inspired by right-winger Garrincha.

Czechoslovakia set a lot of the early running in the tournament and nobody was surprised to see them make the final.

Yet at the Nacional Stadium in Santiago, after Josef Masopust had given the Czechoslovakians the lead, goals from Amarildo, Zito and Vavá helped Brazil to a second successive World Cup title.

1966 ENGLAND
Teams involved: 16
Goals scored: 89
Golden Boot: Eusébio 9
Winners: England

Over 1.5m people attended the 1966 FIFA World Cup™ and most would have been delighted as Sir Alf Ramsey's "Wingless Wonders" lifted the Jules Rimet Trophy in front of a packed and ecstatic Wembley Stadium crowd.

In a tournament that captured the English public's imagination, players like Pelé and Eusébio were in stunning form.

But it was Geoff Hurst's hat-trick in the final against West Germany – which England won 4-2 after extra time – that is best remembered as Hurst and his teammates cemented themselves in English sporting folklore.

MAGIC MEMORIES

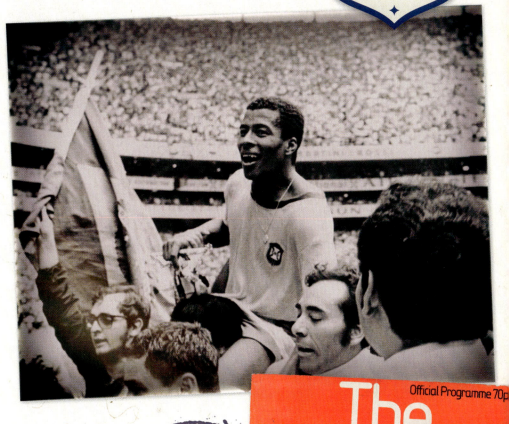

1970 MEXICO
Teams involved: 16
Goals scored: 95
Golden Boot: Gerd Müller (GER) 10
Winners: Brazil

If the 1958 FIFA World Cup™ was the tournament that introduced Pelé to the world, this edition 12 years later was when he enthralled the world.

Brazil were in stunning form at Mexico 1970 and in the red-hot temperatures of the Estadio Azteca, the South Americans were simply too strong for Italy in the final.

Goals from Pelé, Gérson, Jairzinho and Carlos Alberto – the latter's strike being one of the greatest team goals ever seen – helped Brazil to a colourful victory in a colourful tournament.

1974 GERMANY FR
Teams involved: 16
Goals scored: 97
Golden Boot: Grzegorz Lato (POL) 7
Winners: West Germany

This was the tournament where "Total Football" became the biggest talking point and West Germany and the Netherlands, led by the respective brilliance of Franz Beckenbauer and Johan Cruyff, came to the fore.

The Dutch were the favourites but in front of a hugely partisan crowd at the Olympiastadion in Munich, West Germany's mental strength paid off.

An early penalty from Johan Neeskens put the Netherlands ahead but Paul Breitner and Gerd Müller turned the final on its head and ensured West Germany would enjoy glory on home soil.

1978 ARGENTINA
Teams involved: 16
Goals scored: 102
Golden Boot: Mario Kempes (ARG) 6
Winners: Argentina

Argentina had waited 48 years to forget the pain of losing to Uruguay in the very first FIFA World Cup™ final, and in front of their own ecstatic fans they finally lifted the trophy.

At the Estadio Monumental, on a pitch speckled with confetti, the Netherlands lost their second successive final as Golden Boot winner Mario Kempes scored twice and Daniel Bertoni also netted as Ernst Happel's side were defeated 3-1 after extra time.

After watching both Uruguay and Brazil lift the trophy before them, it was time for Argentina to join the South American party.

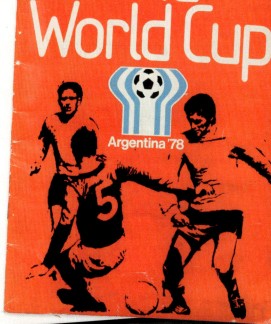

1982 SPAIN
Teams involved: 24
Goals scored: 146
Golden Boot: Paolo Rossi (ITA) 6
Winners: Spain

The first FIFA World Cup™ to involve 24 teams was also the first to witness a goalkeeper lift the trophy as Italy were victorious in Spain.

Dino Zoff was the Italians' legendary goalkeeper and he was at his best as they faced West Germany in the final.

In front of 90,000 fans at the Santiago Bernabéu, goals from Paolo Rossi, Marco Tardelli and Alessandro Altobelli were enough for a 3-1 win against a West German side who had also been impressive throughout the tournament.

MAGIC MEMORIES

1986 MEXICO
Teams involved: 24
Goals scored: 132
Golden Boot: Gary Lineker (ENG) 6
Winners: Argentina

Mexico hosted the FIFA World Cup™ for the second time in 16 years and Argentina's Diego Maradona was the man who dominated from start to finish.

His fame hit new heights in the quarter-final against England, as the infamous "Hand of God" and a wonderful solo effort in a 2-1 win meant few players hit the headlines like Maradona did.

In the final against West Germany at the Estadio Azteca, 114,600 people watched Argentina win 3-2 in a wonderful match that tipped this way and that until Jorge Burruchaga won it for the South Americans with just six minutes to go.

1990 ITALY
Teams involved: 24
Goals scored: 115
Golden Boot: Salvatore Schillaci (ITA) 6
Winners: West Germany

Germany got their revenge on Argentina at the 1990 FIFA World Cup™ in Italy as they came out on top in a tight, tough final at the Stadio Olimpico in Rome.

Paul "Gazza" Gascoigne's tears when England were eliminated in the semi-finals provided an iconic image for a fine tournament but it was the ruthless performance of the West Germans that made all the difference.

In the final, an Andreas Brehme penalty with five minutes remaining was enough for Lothar Matthäus to lift the FIFA World Cup Trophy.

1994 USA
Teams involved: 24
Goals scored: 141
Golden Boot: Oleg Salenko (RUS), Hristo Stoichkov (BUL) 6
Winners: Brazil

The USA joined the FIFA World Cup™ party as the country was selected as hosts for the first time.

The final between Brazil and Italy was a staid affair and eventually led to the first-ever penalty shoot-out to decide the winners, and it was Italy who blinked first as a miss by the legendary Roberto Baggio meant Brazil bagged their fourth FIFA World Cup crown.

Commercially, the tournament was a huge success and an average of nearly 69,000 fans attended the 52 matches.

1998 FRANCE
Teams involved: 32
Goals scored: 171
Golden Boot: Davor Šuker (CRO) 6
Winners: France

The FIFA World Cup™ again grew in size as 32 teams competed for glory in France – and once again the home nation was the country left smiling by the end of the tournament.

This was the second time France had hosted the tournament, while Croatia, Jamaica, Japan and South Africa all took part in their first World Cup.

France and Brazil tussled in the final but the much-fancied South Americans – spearheaded by the wonderfully talented Ronaldo – were shocked as a Zinédine Zidane-inspired performance saw *Les Bleus* crowned as victors in front of an ecstatic 100,000 people in Paris.

MAGIC MEMORIES

2002 KOREA/JAPAN
Teams involved: 32
Goals scored: 161
Golden Boot: Ronaldo (BRA) 8
Winners: Brazil

Brazil had been stunned at the FIFA World Cup™ in 1998, but they would not be denied four years later.

Led again by the indefatigable genius that was Ronaldo, and with further talents such as Ronaldinho and Rivaldo also in good form, Luiz Felipe Scolari's side were just too sharp for Germany in the final.

In front of 69,000 people at the International Stadium Yokohama, a double from Ronaldo sealed a win over Germany, with players such as Roberto Carlos and Cafu also becoming national heroes.

2006 GERMANY
Teams involved: 32
Goals scored: 147
Golden Boot: Miroslav Klose (GER) 5
Winners: Italy

France were desperate to win their second FIFA World Cup™ but Italy proved to be a step too far in Germany.

The final of this captivating tournament was overshadowed by Zinédine Zidane's sending off, and when the game went to extra time and penalties, having finished 1-1, it was Italy who held their nerve.

Fabio Grosso scored the winning spot-kick to give Italy the glory and erase their painful memories of losing the 1994 final in the same manner.

2010 SOUTH AFRICA
Teams involved: 32
Goals scored: 145
Golden Boot: Thomas Müller (GER) 5
Winners: Spain

The first FIFA World Cup™ held on the African continent was a stunning display of passion, colour and – with the ever-present vuvuzela instrument – a cacophony of noise.

Spain underlined their position as the finest team in the world at the time as they played some wonderful football and managed to overcome the Netherlands in a 1-0 victory after extra time as the inspired Andrés Iniesta found the winner in the 116th minute.

Curiously, there was only one unbeaten team at the tournament and it wasn't Spain, who lost their opening group game. Instead, it was New Zealand who exited the World Cup undefeated having drawn all three of their group games.

2014 BRAZIL
Teams involved: 32
Goals scored: 145
Golden Boot: James Rodríguez (COL) 6
Winners: Germany

The FIFA World Cup™ was hosted in Brazil for the second time – after a 64-year wait – and the world was rewarded with a tournament full of colour and wonderful football.

Brazil struggled to perform at their best and were on the wrong end of a stunning semi-final result as Germany crushed them 7-1.

An incredible 3,386,810 supporters watched the 64 matches and the Maracanã was crammed to capacity as Germany repeated their Italia 90 success with another 1-0 win over Argentina thanks to a stunning extra-time goal from the brilliant Mario Götze.

FIFA WORLD FOOTBALL MUSEUM

THE WHOLE FIFA WORLD CUP™ IN ONE BUILDING

The home of the FIFA World Cup Trophy and where the stars visit the 'Wall of Champions'

Here is a question for your football-obsessed friends and family; where in the world can you see the planet's greatest sporting trophy, dance the 'The Cuadrado Zombie shake' and bump into one of your all-time footballing heroes, all under one roof?

The answer is simple – and magnificent. To do all of the above, and much, much more, head for the FIFA World Football Museum in Zurich, Switzerland.

With its wonderfully angular and artistic shape, the FIFA World Football Museum is an interactive delight that entertains and educates people of all ages.

And, alongside stars like Cafu, Miroslav Klose and Joachim Löw, you will not be disappointed if you pay a visit.

The museum opened its doors in February 2016 after a twenty months construction phase and is so well-equipped for life in the 21st century that it is actually linked to Lake Zurich and uses water from the lake as a source of energy that helps to heat the building in winter and cool it down in the summer.

Yet it is not the building's environmental prowess that sees 10,000 visitors a month pass through the doors. No, the reason so many people travel to Tessinerplatz is to wander through and absorb the treasures contained inside and to see the hundreds of items that chronicle, celebrate and commemorate the game of football.

And as befitting the world's largest sporting tournament, it is only right that a huge part of the FIFA World Football Museum is dedicated to celebrating the FIFA World Cup™ with the famous trophy itself being one of the true highlights.

Since the 1974 finals in West Germany the champions have been given their own replica of the trophy to keep - the 'Winner's Trophy' - with the actual trophy being kept by FIFA in a bank vault in Zurich, only seen by the public in the lead-up and during the final tournament.

However, since 2016, fans from across the globe can see the FIFA World Cup Trophy in all its glory in the museum, where it is the centrepiece exhibit. It's a common sight to see visitors crowded around it with huge smiles on their faces, aware that they are looking at the

FIFA WORLD FOOTBALL MUSEUM

most iconic and recognised sporting trophy in the world.

In the main exhibition hall, football fans can also wander at their leisure through the FIFA World Cup Gallery with every edition of the tournament celebrated and marked with original objects and displays that tell the story of the winners and losers throughout the past nine decades.

Other historical documents in the FIFA World Football Museum include Sir Stanley Rous' handwritten draft of the Laws of the Game, published in 1936, the minute book from the International FA Board meeting in 1913 when FIFA formally joined football's supreme law-making body, and the lapis lazuli base of the original World Cup trophy, the Jules Rimet Cup™.

However, one of the FIFA World Football Museum's biggest strengths is the superb way it combines the old with the new and for the 21st century generation of football fans, there is more to the museum's attractions, in addition to the historical artefacts.

Young visitors, in particular, can be tested and taught about football in a number of ways. There are many interactive displays that talk visitors through the balls used at the World Cup since 1930, different shirts and kits, the posters that have advertised the tournament through the years and videos and interactive images of some of the greatest matches in World Cup history.

People can also try their hand at being a referee, where their decision making and calm approach are tested to the limits, they can show off their broadcasting skills as they commentate on a football match and they can also show off their dance skills as they attempt

England World Cup winner Roger Hunt holds the Jules Rimet Cup™ again

The Swiss national women's football team use the museum's photo booth

5 FASCINATING FIFA WORLD FOOTBALL MUSEUM OBJECTS

1. JULES RIMET CUP™

Of the mysteries surrounding the theft of great works of art, the story of the Jules Rimet Cup™ is up there with the best of them - as famous as the disappearance of the Amber Room from St Petersburg during the war, or the Gardner museum heist of 1990 in which Rembrandt's *Christ in the Storm on the Lake of Galilee* was stolen along with 12 other priceless works. When, in 1970, Brazil won the FIFA World Cup for the third time, they were given the Jules Rimet Cup™ to keep. By then it had already attained iconic status. For 13 years it was on display at the headquarters of the CBF in Rio de Janeiro before it was stolen on the night of 19 December 1983. Doubts were quickly cast on the official police story that the trophy had been melted down, but efforts to find the trophy in the 35 years since have proved fruitless. Apart, that is, from the extraordinary discovery in 2014 of the original lapis lazuli base. Sculpted by Abel Lafleur in 1929, it was replaced in 1958 by a bigger base on which more winners could be inscribed. This Lafleur base is one of the star exhibits in the FIFA museum and sits underneath a silver and gold plated replica discovered at the same time as the base.

2. LEONIDAS MEDAL

Brazil's Leonidas da Silva was one of the first great heroes of the World Cup. The top scorer at the 1938 finals in France, he was known as "O Diamante Negro" - the Black Diamond - and is one of a number of players credited with having invented the bicycle kick, a technique he first used in a league match in 1932. He died in 2004 at the age of 90 but had long been suffering from the effects of Alzheimer's. His wife, Albertina Pereira dos Santos, had nursed him through his final days while faithfully preserving mementos and artefacts from his career. Chief amongst those was this medal from the 1938 World Cup which she donated to the FIFA Museum and which takes pride of place in the showcase dedicated to the tournament. The Brazilians finished third but this was in the days before bronze medals were awarded and so this is a participation medal which was given to every player taking part in the finals. A fitting tribute to one of the all-time greats.

FIFA WORLD FOOTBALL MUSEUM

Brazilian star Cafu next to the FIFA World Cup Trophy

one of 12 goalscoring celebrations, from the 'The Cuadrado Zombie shake' to 'The Swedish Swing'.

The 2018 FIFA World Cup™ will undoubtedly put the FIFA World Football Museum in the spotlight and while every new guest is a welcome face, FIFA have also reached out and invited a number of extra-special guests since it opened to allow them a very emotional, and personal, experience at the museum's 'Wall of Champions'. This contains the name of every single one of the 422 players and 19 coaches who have won the World Cup. All of those still alive, and who come to the museum, are invited to sign the wall for posterity. They also get to recreate a very special and emotional moment as they once again get their hands on the FIFA World Cup Trophy.

Only former winners and heads of state are allowed to touch the Trophy – even FIFA's own museum staff do not touch it. The first to sign the Wall of Champions was Brazil's Jose Altafini, a winner in 1958, while others have included Christian Karembeu from 1998 and 1966 winner Roger Hunt among others.

One former winner, Christoph Kramer – who was successful four years ago with Germany – visited the museum on his own, very quietly queued for a ticket and was then recognised by staff who organised an impromptu signing session.

Famous football personalities visit the museum regularly, meaning visitors always have the chance of meeting one of their idols.

For those of us not blessed with having won a World Cup, the museum also holds plenty of cultural events such as panel discussions, lectures, film screenings, temporary exhibitions, public tours and literature evenings.

In short, there is something inside the FIFA World Football Museum that will entertain, captivate and inform everybody.

2018 is already a wonderful year for football fans around the world and a visit to the FIFA World Football Museum can only make that year even better.

For more information visit: www.fifamuseum.com

3. ADEMIR'S BOOTS

We live in an era now where players have boot contracts worth millions and have the boots specially designed and made, often with their names as part of the design for marketing purposes. So it's sobering to know that the top scorer at the 1950 World Cup used a hammer and a nail to write his name on his boots, not for promotional purposes but because he was concerned someone might steal them! The letters of his name are etched just below the ankle collar of each boot. Ademir scored eight goals at the finals in his home country wearing these boots, a feat which meant he also joined Guillermo Stábile and Leonidas as the all-time record scorer - a position all three held until four years later.

4. KREITLEIN'S ARCHIVE

Ever wondered where red and yellow cards came from? Well, they have their origin in the England - Argentina match at the 1966 World Cup refereed by Rudolf Kreitlein. It was a bad tempered match in which Argentina's Antonio Rattín was sent off by Kreitlein, events recorded in his notebook which is on display at the FIFA Museum, along with the whistle he used and the ball. During the match there was great confusion as to what was going on when Rattín was sent off. Watching the game was Ken Aston, the head of the FIFA referees' department, who on the way home had a eureka moment. As he approached a set of traffic lights they turned to yellow and then red. The idea of a yellow card to indicate a booking, and a red card to indicate that a player had been sent off was born.

5. PELÉ'S TRACKSUIT

One of the most iconic artefacts in the FIFA Museum is the tracksuit worn by the 17-year-old Pelé at the 1958 World Cup in Sweden. Pelé was a popular figure during the finals and wherever he went, he was photographed talking to the locals, often in this distinctive tracksuit, which doubled as training gear and everyday wear. The Brazilians came prepared for a Northern European summer: the tracksuit was made of wool! Pelé remains one of the most famous players of all-time. In the semi-final against France that year he scored a hat-trick, the last Brazilian to do so at a World Cup. Since then 28 hat-tricks have been scored at the 14 World Cups played, but none of them by a Brazilian!

2018 FIFA World Cup™ Official Sponsor

POWER OF NATURE BORN FOR GREATNESS

REFEREES

The best of the refs

They will run over 12 kilometres in every match, they have some massive decisions to make, they need to stay cool, calm and focused at all times and they need to be able to handle intense pressure. Yet we are not talking about the 22 stars on show in every FIFA World Cup™ match.

No, instead, we are discussing the referees who will be in charge at the tournament.

It is so easy to overlook the unique contribution a referee makes to a football match but, quite literally, they are the most important person on the pitch.

Without the man with the whistle, the FIFA World Cup could not take place.

FIFA has selected 36 referees from all over the planet for the 2018 FIFA World Cup™ and they all met in Abu Dhabi in November last year for a five-day seminar designed to help them prepare for a tournament where they will be under an enormous amount of scrutiny and where their officiating skills will be tested to the very limits.

"We're always looking to improve and we'll work hard to be as prepared as we possibly can be for the World Cup," said Pierluigi Collina, the legendary Italian referee who officiated the 2002 FIFA World Cup™ final between Brazil and Germany and is now the chairman of the FIFA Referees Committee.

Under the bright blue skies of the United Arab Emirates, the referees were put through their physical paces to ensure they are in top condition for the arduous task of refereeing such a high-paced sport, and Collina and his coaches also helped the officials work on their decision-making, their positioning on the pitch as well as their body language and communication skills so they can continually improve the job they do in the middle.

"FIFA competitions attract a lot of attention and that creates a lot of pressure," Collina added. "The referee is always in charge of what happens on the pitch."

The Italian is right to remind everybody of the importance of the refereeing team in every footballing contest – no matter the level – and what is clear is that the referees at the 2018 FIFA World Cup will be better prepared, fitter and more experienced than ever before.

2014 FIFA World Cup™ final referee Nicola Rizzoli

FIFA WORLD CUP™ FINAL REFEREES

1930	John Langenus (Belgium)
1934	Ivan Eklind (Sweden)
1938	Georges Capdeville (France)
1950	George Reader (England)
1954	William Ling (England)
1958	Maurice Guigue (France)
1962	Nikolay Latyshev (Soviet Union)
1966	Gottfried Dienst (Switzerland)
1970	Rudi Glöckner (East Germany)
1974	Jack Taylor (England)
1978	Sergio Gonella (Italy)
1982	Arnaldo Cézar Coelho (Brazil)
1986	Romualdo Arppi Filho (Brazil)
1990	Edgardo Codesal (Mexico)
1994	Sándor Puhl (Hungary)
1998	Said Belqola (Morocco)
2002	Pierluigi Collina (Italy)
2006	Horacio Elizondo (Argentina)
2010	Howard Webb (England)
2014	Nicola Rizzoli (Italy)

OFFICIAL SMARTPHONE

X21

IN-DISPLAY FINGERPRINT SCANNING
PERFECT SHOT, EVEN WITH BACKLIHT

A global smartphone brand focusing on introducing perfect sound quality and ultimate photography with cutting-edge technology, Vivo develops dynamic and stylish products for passionate young people. Vivo makes stylish smartphones with cutting-edge technology accessible to young people and professionals around the world. We now have close to two hundred million users to date and is one of the preferred brands of young people around the world. As an Official Sponsor of the FIFA World Cup™, Vivo believes in the importance of encouraging young people to embrace self-expression and an energetic lifestyle.

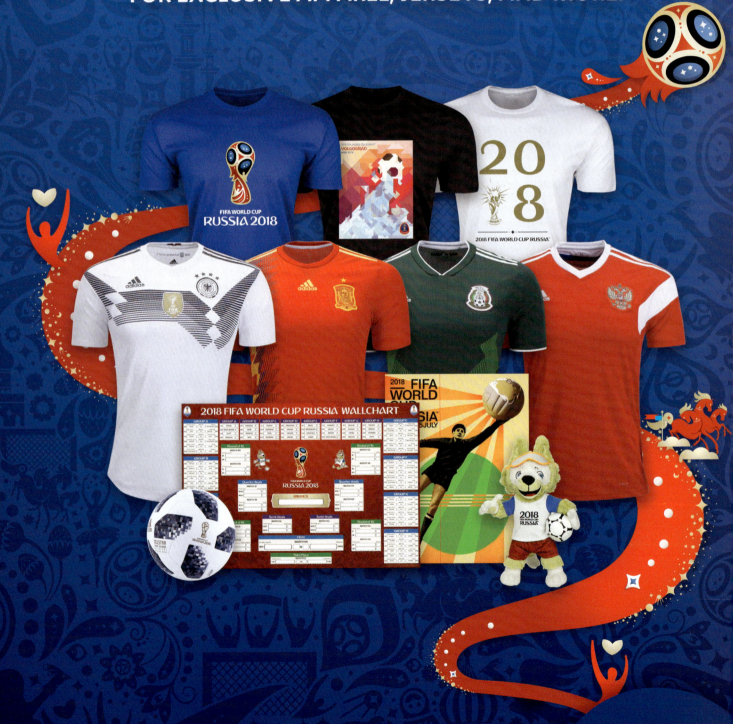

MASCOT

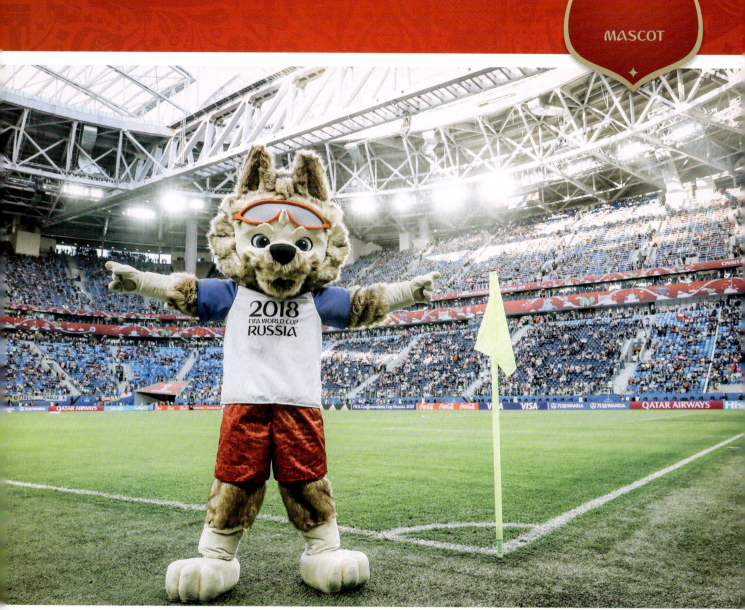

Adding extra fun to football's biggest occasion

What do the names Zabivaka™, Goleo VI™ and Zakumi™ and all have in common?

That's right, they are the public face and the public fun of FIFA World Cup™ tournaments through the ages and have all enjoyed their moment in the spotlight as an Official Mascot.

For the 2018 FIFA World Cup Russia™, the selection of Zabivaka, a funky looking wolf with red shorts, a blue and white T-shirt, a mean right-foot shot and a big grin on his face, came after plenty of consultation.

Zabivaka's colours represent the Russian flag and he was designed to be a friendly and welcoming face for the biggest football tournament on the planet.

When World Cup Willie – the first World Cup mascot – was designed for the 1966 edition in England, he was simply drawn by a children's illustrator but since then, the process of selecting an Official Mascot has become far more interactive and inclusive.

Zabivaka was the brainchild of Russian design student Ekaterina Bocharova, who put her creation forward for the official vote and was thrilled to see Zabivaka chosen after a million Russian football fans selected him in an online poll.

Zabivaka's name means "the one who scores" in Russian and he picked up 53 per cent of the votes.

"I imagine that I will see him on keyrings and on fridge magnets," Bocharova said. "And I will remember that I created him and I will be proud of myself."

And so she should be!

Brazilian great Ronaldo agrees that no FIFA World Cup is complete without its Official Mascot.

"Mascots are great ambassadors for promoting the event and bring so much joy to the stadiums," he said. "I can see it happening already in Russia with Zabivaka. He will surely be remembered for a very long time to come by football fans all over the world."

FIFA.com

IT'S ALL ABOUT THE BALL

When the whistle blows and the 2018 FIFA World Cup™ gets underway in spectacular fashion in Russia, it would be easy for fans across the globe to get carried away by the magnificent stadiums, the colourful supporters, the passion on display in the stands and on the pitch, and all the fireworks which surround such an incredible event.

Yet what should not be forgotten is that the smallest part of the jigsaw that helps make a FIFA World Cup™ match so special is also the most important part. We are, of course, talking about the football itself.

Since the 1970 FIFA World Cup™, adidas have been tasked with creating the footballs for the tournament, and the ball chosen for the 2018 edition is likely to remain as memorable as all the rest.

Messi in action with the Telstar 18

In a throwback to the first ball they designed, adidas have created the Telstar 18, a ball that looks remarkably similar to the iconic black-and-white patched ball from that wonderful Mexico tournament.

Made from 32 panels, the original Telstar ball had 12 black panels that ball designers at the time believed would help the ball be easier to spot on the black-and-white televisions that were prevalent at the time.

The balls used since the Telstar – such as the Tango España (Spain 1982), Azteca (Mexico 1986) and Teamgeist (Germany 2006) – have always incorporated a sense of those first epic black-and-white markings, and the Telstar 18 certainly continues that tradition.

"The Telstar 18 evokes unforgettable memories of the 1970 FIFA World Cup – and of legends like Pelé, Gerd Müller, Giacinto Facchetti, Pedro Rocha and Bobby Moore – and will feed the dreams of those who will play for football's most coveted prize," a FIFA spokesperson said.

Roland Rommler, Category Director of Football Hardware at adidas, added: "The original Telstar is one of the most iconic footballs of all time and one which changed football design forever, so developing the Telstar 18 while staying true to the original model was a really exciting challenge for us.

"The new panel structure and inclusion of an NFC chip has taken football innovation and design to a new level and offers both consumers and players a completely new experience."

The ball was unveiled in Moscow in November last year and immediately received the thumbs-up from football stars past and present.

And if it is good enough for Lionel Messi, Argentina's genius, then it should be good enough for everyone. "I was lucky enough to get to know this ball a bit earlier and I managed to have a try with it," said Messi. "I like all of it: the new design, the colours, everything."

Before adidas were tasked with creating an official football for the FIFA World Cup, earlier tournaments took an ad hoc approach to what type of ball they used and who designed them. In fact, during the very first FIFA World Cup final in Uruguay, the ball for the first half – the Tiento – was supplied by Argentina while Uruguay supplied the ball for the second half – the T-Model – because it was felt that it was fair for both sides to use a ball of their choosing!

As the FIFA World Cup grew in stature, balls such as the Allen (France 1938) and Duplo T (Brazil 1950) became increasingly technical as balls began to be stitched together rather than laced tightly, and they were also by no means just white as the Swiss World Champion (Switzerland 1954) and Crack (Chile 1962) were both yellow.

Perhaps the most memorable early ball was the brightly coloured Challenge 4-star created by Slazenger for the 1966 FIFA World Cup™ in England. It was certainly an iconic moment when Geoff Hurst completed his hat-trick by firing into the top corner against West Germany in the final and, at that moment in time, it looked as if golden orange footballs would be the future of FIFA World Cup finals.

However, along came the stunningly manufactured and simply beautiful Telstar in 1970 to change FIFA World Cup balls forever.

BALL HISTORY

1930	1934	1938	1950	1954	1958	1962	1966	1970	1974
T-Model	Federale 102	Allen	Superball Duplo T	Swiss World Champion	Top Star	Crack	Slazenger Challenge	Adidas Telstar Durlast	Adidas Telstar Durlast

THE BALL

BALL HISTORY

1978
Adidas Tango Durlast

1982
Adidas Tango España

1986
Adidas Azteca

1990
Adidas Etrusco Unico

1994
Adidas Questra

1998
Adidas Tricolore

2002
Adidas Fevernova

2006
Adidas Teamgeist

2010
Adidas Jabulani

2014
Adidas Brazuca

BE THERE IN STYLE

2018 FIFA WORLD CUP RUSSIA™
OFFICIAL HOSPITALITY PROGRAMME

As FIFA gears up for the most important event on its calendar,
it's your chance to experience the world's favourite football tournament in style.

With limited packages still available for key matches,
take a look at our latest selection of Official Hospitality products and buy yours today,
to ensure that you witness history in the making.

fifa.com/Hospitality

Be welcomed by MATCH Hospitality hostesses | Catering service matching the level of hospitality purchased | Guaranteed match-day ticket, without any draw or lotto | Complimentary commemorative gift | Excellent beverage service | Best available seats in your hospitality category | Parking available on request for hospitality customers | Exclusive entrance and welcome desk for hospitality clients on match day

FIFA WORLD CUP™ WISDOM

Test your knowledge of the 20 FIFA World Cup™ events so far...

1. Uruguay won the first edition of FIFA World Cup™ in 1930, but in which South American country were the finals held?

2. Which Croatian won the Golden Boot at the 1998 FIFA World Cup France™?

3. During the 1958 tournament in Sweden, Brazil won both the semi-final and final 5-2 against France and Sweden respectively. Altogether, how many goals did Pele score in those two games – 3, 4 or 5?

4. The mascot for the 1982 FIFA World Cup™ in Spain was called Naranjito. What type of fruit did it resemble?

5. The 1950 edition of FIFA World Cup™ was the first time which of these countries had competed in the World Cup finals – England, Chile, Spain or the USA?

6. Which team became the first European nation to win the FIFA World Cup™ outside of Europe?

Pelé hit the goal trail at the 1958 FIFA World Cup™

7. The 1970 FIFA World Cup™ in Mexico will forever be remembered for the wonderful Brazil side that won the competition, but which German finished as top goalscorer in the tournament?

8. In 1990, which African team beat holders Argentina in the opening match of the tournament?

9. Which European nation did Italy beat in the final to win 1938 FIFA World Cup™?

10. Three South American teams took part in the 1978 FIFA World Cup™. Brazil and Argentina were two of them. Which was the other?

11. The 2006 FIFA World Cup™ saw defenders score both the first and last goals of the tournament. Marco Materazzi scored the final goal for Italy, but which German scored the opening goal of the first game?

A defender started the scoring at the 2006 FIFA World Cup™

QUIZ

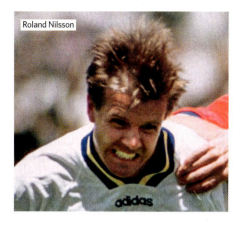
Roland Nilsson

12. The 1962 FIFA World Cup™ in Chile saw one British team take part. Which one?

13. The captains of the two teams that contested the third-place play-off match at the 1994 FIFA World Cup USA™ were Roland Nilsson and Borislav Mikhailov. Which two countries were they representing?

14. Italy won the 1934 FIFA World Cup™, but the top goalscorer was Oldřich Nejedlý, who scored five goals for the runners-up. Which country did he represent?

15. England hosted and won the 1966 FIFA World Cup™, but which Portuguese star finished as the tournament's top goalscorer?

16. At the 2002 FIFA World Cup™ in Korea Republic and Japan, the reigning champions, France, were beaten 1-0 in their opening game by an African nation making their first-ever World Cup finals appearance. Which country was that?

17. The final of the 1954 FIFA World Cup™ was dubbed the "Miracle of Bern", but which two European teams took part?

Diego Maradona took centre stage in the quarter-final between Argentina and England at the 1986 FIFA World Cup™

18. The quarter-final match at the 1986 FIFA World Cup Mexico™ between Argentina and England ended 2-1 to the South Americans and is remembered for two goals by Diego Maradona – the "Hand of God" goal and a terrific solo effort. But who scored England's goal?

19. Carlos Caszely became the first player to be sent off during a World Cup finals match when he was shown a red card in 1974. Which South American country did he represent?

20. Thomas Müller was the second highest goalscorer at the 2014 FIFA World Cup Brazil™, but which Colombian claimed the Golden Boot with six goals?

France made a bad start at the 2002 FIFA World Cup™

ANSWERS

1. Uruguay, 2. Davor Šuker, 3. 5 (3 against France, 2 against Sweden), 4. Orange, 5. England, 6. Spain in 2010 in South Africa, 7. Gerd Müller, 8. Cameroon, 9. Hungary, 10. Peru, 11. Philipp Lahm, 12. England, 13. Sweden and Bulgaria, 14. Czechoslovakia, 15. Eusébio, 16. Senegal, 17. West Germany beat Hungary 3-2, 18. Gary Lineker, 19. Chile, 20. James Rodríguez.